JN084349

NHK
WORLD
JAPAN

NHK
NEWSLINE

5

Tatsuroh Yamazaki
Stella M. Yamazaki

KINSEIDO

Kinseido Publishing Co., Ltd.

3-21 Kanda Jimbo-cho, Chiyoda-ku,

Tokyo 101-0051, Japan

First published 2022 by Kinseido Publishing Co., Ltd.

Video materials NHK (Japan Broadcasting Corporation)

Authors and publisher are grateful to NHK Global Media Services, Inc. and all the interviewees who appeared on the news.

はじめに

　NHK NEWSLINE のテキストシリーズが刊行されてから、本書で 5 冊目を迎えることができた。これもみなさまのご支援によるもので心より感謝申し上げる。

　日本社会全体、特に経済界から英語が使えるグローバルな人材育成が求められているのは周知のとおりである。これを受けて文科省は英語民間試験導入を念頭におき、共通テストで英語教育の再生（特に Speaking と Writing 技能の底上げ）を図った。残念ながら、受験生の地域格差や経済格差の問題が解決せず、さらにコロナ禍の影響もあって英語民間試験導入は見送られた。

　その結果、根本的な英語 4 技能の評価法は個別の大学に委ねるというかたちになっているが、国際的に「英語が使える」人材育成は急務であり、グローバルなコミュニケーション手段として確固たる地位を築いた英語の重要性は日々増すばかりであると言える。

　新型コロナウイルス感染拡大によるパンデミックで、都市部の多くの大学などはオンライン授業が主流になっている。しかし、外出自粛要請が継続される中、それを逆手にとって今は自宅でじっくり実力を養う好機ととらえることもできる。オンラインの英会話レッスンは、安全にしてかつ効果が期待できる。それと並行して、会話の前提となるリスニング能力を伸ばす本書のような教材も積極的に活用できる。

　会話は音声のインプットとアウトプットの合わせ技だが、外国語は徹底的に聞いて模倣するという姿勢が常に必要である。従って伝統的な反復練習や文型練習は、語学学習者にとって必修である。目で追うだけではなく何回か反復して「音読」しておこう。音読しておけば記憶に定着しやすく、会話でもとっさの時に出てくるという利点がある。学習者にとって外国語の会話は（運動競技と同様に）スキルであり、練習によって積み上げた「記憶」が頼りなのである。

　本書はリスニングを中心課題に据えたニュースの視聴覚教材である。ニュースは NHK 海外向け放送の NEWSLINE から採択し、適切な長さに編集した。この番組は現代日本の主な出来事や経済、文化、科学の最近の動向などを簡潔にまとめており好評を博している。

　語学は授業中の学習だけではじゅうぶんではない。現在、ニュース映像がオンラインで視聴可能となった。自宅で納得するまで繰り返し見てほしい。その際、まず完成したスクリプト（News Story の穴埋め問題終了後）を見ながら音声と意味の対応を頭に入れ、その後は文字を見ないで聞くという作業が必要である。この繰り返しが何回かあれば、文字なしで映像音声の理解ができるという快感が味わえるようになる。

　末筆ながら、本書の作成に関して金星堂編集部をはじめ関係スタッフの方々に大変お世話になった。更に出版にあたって NHK、株式会社 NHK グローバルメディアサービスの皆様にも映像提供などで御協力をいただいた。ここに厚くお礼を申し上げる。

2022 年 1 月　　　　　　　　　　　　　編著者：山﨑達朗／ Stella M. Yamazaki

本書の構成とねらい

　本書は全部で 15 単元 (units) からなり、各単元とも、①日本語のイントロダクション、② Words & Phrases、③ Before You Watch、④ Watch the News、⑤ Understand the News、⑥ News Story、⑦ Review the Key Expressions、⑧ Discussion Questions という構成になっている。このうち①と②は説明で、③〜⑧が練習問題である。

① 日本語のイントロダクション

この短い日本語の説明（140 字前後）は、ニュースの要点を把握することを目的としている。外国語のリスニングには、何がどのように飛び出してくるかわからないという緊張と不安が常に伴うので、このように限られた背景知識（background knowledge）でも、予め準備があると安心感が出るものである。

② Words & Phrases

比較的難しいか、カギになる語彙や熟語などを学習する。ここで意味的、文法的知識をつけておけば、ニュースを聞いた場合に戸惑いは少なくなる。必要に応じて簡単な例文も入れてある。

③ Before You Watch

ニュース映像を見る前に、その予備知識を獲得したり話題を膨らませたりする意味で単元ごとに違った課題が用意してある。内容としては、日常会話表現の学習であったり、社会・文化に特有な語彙を英語でどう言うかといった課題であったりする。方法としても活動に興味が持てるように、ややゲーム的な要素も入れるようにしてある。英語の語彙を縦横に並んだアルファベット表から見つけ出すタスクや、クロスワードの活用もその例である。

④ Watch the News — First Viewing

ここで初めてクラスで映像を見るわけだが、課題はニュース内容の大きな流れや要点の理解が主となる基本的把握である。設問が 3 つあり、各問とも内容に合っていれば T（= True）、合っていなければ F（= False）を選択し、問題文の真偽を判断する。外国語のリスニングはしぜんに耳から入ってくるということがないので、集中して聞く必要がある。必要に応じて随時、視聴の回数を増やしたり、問題と関連する箇所を教師が集中的に見せたりするということが過去の経験から有効である。

⑤ Understand the News — Second Viewing

同じニュース映像をもう一度見るが、内容についてのやや詳細な質問となっている。次の2種類の下位区分がある。ここも必要に応じ、複数回のリスニングを考慮してほしい。

1 最初の視聴と比べて今度は選択肢が3つになっており、内容もより詳細にわたる設問が用意してある。各問、右端の3枚の写真は、参考にはなるが、問題を解く上でリスニングのキーとなる部分の映像とは限らないので注意してほしい。

2 単元によって、何種類か様々な形式の設問が用意してある。いずれもニュース内容や単語の用法の確認を目的としている。例えばニュースのまとめとなる「概要」や「入手情報の順序づけ」、要点となる数字の記入などである。さらに、設問によっては、ややゲーム的な要素を考慮し、アルファベットの並べ替え (unscrambling) を入れている。

⑥ News Story

これはニュース映像に対応するスクリプトであるが、完全なものにするには「穴埋め問題」を解く必要がある。問題は合計7問で、各問題に6箇所位の空所がある。解答するには、スタジオでややゆっくり読まれた音声CDをクラスで（各2回繰り返し）聞きながら書き取り作業 (dictation) をする。スクリプトのそれぞれの問題には、右端におおよその日本語訳（数字以外）が付けてあるのでヒントになる。書き取りが完成すればニュース映像の全文が目で確かめられるが、スクリプトは映像を見る前に読むことはせず、まず何回か視聴して上記④と⑤の設問に解答した後に、この穴埋めに挑戦してほしい。

⑦ Review the Key Expressions

ここでは、映像で出てきた単語や熟語などのうち応用性のある表現に習熟することがねらいである。そのような重要表現の意味や用法を確実にするとともに、英作文があまり負担なく身につくように単語を与える「整序問題」形式（4問）を採用した。ただし選択肢の中に錯乱肢 (distractors) を1語入れ、適度に難しくしてある。文例は当該単元の話題とは関係なく、いろいろな場面の設定になっている。

⑧ Discussion Questions

最後の問題として、クラス内での話し合いに使える話題を2つ用意してある。当該単元に関連した身近な話題が提示してあるので、短く簡単な英語で自分の考えを表現してみる、というのがねらいである。（ご指導の先生方へ：クラスによっては宿題として、話すことを次回までに考えておくというスタンスでもよいと思われる。この話し合いの課題は、人数や時間などクラス設定との兼ね合いから、用途に応じて柔軟に扱うのがよいと考えられる。）

NHK NEWSLINE 5

Contents

The Challenges of Teaching English amid Coronavirus

コロナ禍で模索する英語教育

コロナ禍で教育現場が苦戦している。生徒どうしの英語のコミュニケーション活動がかなり制限された状態で授業を行っている。長時間のグループ活動や近距離での対話練習は行わない、さらに教師の準備・授業の負担も考慮しなければならない。一方、こういう時こそ我々が変革を生み出す機会なのだと考える人もいる。

THE CHALLENGES OF TEACHING ENGLISH AMID CORONAVIRUS

● Words & Phrases

CD 02

☐ to **work out** （問題）を解決する、丸くおさめる

☐ **silver lining** 明るい希望、前途の光明

☐ **face shield** フェイスシールド

☐ **face-to-face** 向かい合わせで（の）、対面で（の）

☐ **transmission** 感染

☐ to **figure out** ～を解決する、理解する

☐ **patchwork** 寄せ集め

☐ to **hand in** ～を提出する

   Please *hand in* your paper by the end of next week.
   来週の終わりまでにレポートを提出してください。

☐ to **minimize** ～を最小にする

☐ **on track** 順調に進んで、正しく軌道に乗って

   We all hope the economy will get back *on track*.
   経済が再び順調にいくことをみんな願っている。

1 ～ 11 の空所に当てはまる英語を下のアルファベット表から見つけ、線で囲みましょう。
囲み方は縦、横いずれも可能で、太字で始まる単語がヒントになるかもしれません。

例: (**Attention**   ), everyone.   こちらを見てください、みなさん。

1. Come to the (   ).   前に出てきてください。

2. Write your answer on the (   ).   （黒）板に答えを書いてください。

3. It's okay to make (   ).《複数形》   間違えても大丈夫です。

4. Take your (   ).   じっくりやってください。

5. Your answer is (   ). Try again.   答えは惜しいです。もう一度やりましょう。

6. Well (   ).   よくできました。

7. Give him/her a big (   ).   彼／彼女に拍手をお願いします。

8. Sit together in (   ).《複数形》   ペアになってすわってください。

9. (   ) each other.   向き合ってください。

10. Please take one (   ) each.   各自、プリントを 1 枚取ってください。

11. Pass the rest (   ).   残りは後ろに回して［送って］ください。

	1	2	3	4	5	6	7	8	9	10	11	12	13
a	A	T	T	E	N	T	I	O	N	T	B	H	P
b	R	M	I	S	T	A	K	E	S	I	E	A	A
c	D	O	C	L	O	S	E	B	S	M	S	N	I
d	O	M	I	D	D	L	E	A	T	E	T	D	R
e	N	T	B	O	A	R	D	C	O	L	D	O	S
f	E	Z	H	A	N	D	Q	K	P	R	O	U	T
g	F	A	C	E	A	I	F	R	O	N	T	T	A

ニュースを見て、内容と合っているものは T、違っているものは F を選びましょう。

1. Many Japanese schools had been closed for four months before they opened again. [T / F]

2. Teachers are working hard to come up with their own safe and effective techniques.

[T / F]

3. Teachers say that online English education is the best solution for the time being. [T / F]

1 ニュースをもう一度見て、各問の空所に入る適切な選択肢を a 〜 c から選びましょう。

1. Many students are afraid of _____.
   a. talking to native speakers of English
   b. removing their masks if they sit close
   c. speaking English due to bad pronunciation

2. Mr. Kawano says he'll try hard to find solutions _____.
   a. but there are few useful strategies
   b. because there are a lot of possibilities
   c. although he has a limited budget

3. Videos help the teacher to _____.
   a. encourage his students to talk louder
   b. spend more time on his students' homework
   c. speak less in the classroom

2 右の文字列を並べ替えて単語を作り、各文の空所に入れて意味がとおるようにしましょう。

1. According to a proverb, "Every cloud has a (   ) lining."   [lersiv]

2. Some workers wear both a mask and a face (   ) to protect against the virus.   [dlishe]

3. The teacher could not (   ) out what strategy would work best for teaching online.   [reguif]

4. The teacher asked the students to (   ) in their iPads containing their assignments.   [dhna]

3 CD の音声を聞いて、次ページ News Story の❶〜❼の文中にある空所に適切な単語を書き入れましょう。音声は 2 回繰り返されます。   ◎ CD 03

Anchor: Next, many schools here in Japan recently welcomed back students after closing for months due to the coronavirus. Teachers are now **working out** how to keep them safe, especially in English classes. But as NHK World's Yamamoto
5 Saori reports, there could be a **silver lining**.

Narrator: The coronavirus is changing the face of education. ❶ This is what you can expect to see at Japanese schools, but it
(¹) (²) (³)
(⁴) (⁵) (⁶) where
10 conversation is key.

Teacher: Okay, so please *wear**¹ your **face shield**.

Narrator: ❷ This English teacher at a public junior high school in Tokyo doesn't let students sit **face-to-face** and avoids group work (¹) (²) (³)
15 (⁴) (⁵) (⁶). And then there are the face shields.

He thought it would be easier to check pronunciation if he could see the students' faces, but many are afraid to take off their mask[s]*² when there isn't much social distancing.

20 ❸ The teacher says (¹) (²)
(³) (⁴) (⁵).

Kawano Mitsushi (English teacher): I feel like I'm juggling two things, education and preventing **transmission**, that are almost impossible to deal with at the same time. I'll do my best to
25 **figure out** what works, although the options are limited.

Reporter (Yamamoto Saori): The education ministry has issued guidelines to deal with the virus, but teachers are also developing their own solutions, leading to a **patchwork** of different measures.

❶ 語学学習では
さらに複雑に
なる

❷ 感染の危険を
制限する

❸ 難しい挑戦に
直面している

Teachers at this school are taking [a]*³ more high tech approach.

❹ On the stairs and in the hallways, students (¹)
(²) (³) (⁴)
(⁵) (⁶) but with iPads. The
devices allow them to get away from their desks and stay a safe
distance from each other. ❺ They record themselves speaking
and then **hand in** iPads (¹) (²)
(³) (⁴) (⁵)
(⁶) (⁷).

Teacher: (*On the screen*) Hello, everyone. This is Tou-Tube channel.
Now, let's start English class.

Narrator: The teacher is also making videos to help **minimize** how
much he has to talk.

Sato Akihito (English teacher): Complaining about what we cannot
do doesn't help anything. We should instead think about what
we can do.

Narrator: This expert hopes innovation[s]*⁴ like these will shape the
future of public schooling in the country.

Torikai Kumiko (Professor Emeritus, Rikkyo University): Teachers
now have a chance to think about what they want students to
learn the most. ❻ (¹) (²)
(³) (⁴) (⁵)
(⁶) (⁷) to create a new style of
education.

Narrator: ❼ After losing a lot of class hours to the pandemic, teachers
are trying to get back **on track** with new educational strategies
(¹) (²) (³)
(⁴) (⁵) (⁶).
Yamamoto Saori, NHK World, Tokyo.

❹ マスク無しで
英語の発音の
練習をする

❺ 先生が生徒た
ち［彼ら］の
勉強を調べる
ことができる

❻ 世界的な伝染
病が大きな好
機になりうる

❼ （それが）安
全で役に立つ

Notes

*¹ 動作を表す put on が適切

*² -s が必要

*³ a が必要

*⁴ -s が必要

Review the Key Expressions

各問、選択肢から適切な単語を選び、英文を完成させましょう。なお、余分な単語が1語
ずつあります。

1. そのベンチャー企業は、チームの頑張りのおかげで大きな成功を収めた。

The venture (   ) (   ) a big success (_____)

(_____) the (   ) hard (   ).

> to   business   team's   work   achieved   of   due

2. 一年以上のオンライン授業を行った後、以前の対面（の）授業がいかに効率的だったか、
ありがたさがよくわかる。

Now we really (   ) how (   ) old (_____)-to-face

classes (   ) after (   ) (   ) a year in online

classes.

> over   efficient   face   mask   appreciate   spending   were

3. 長い間付き合っていたのに、なぜガールフレンドが会ってくれなくなったのか理解で
きない。

I can't (_____) (_____) why my girlfriend (   )

(   ) me after we (   ) been (   ) so long.

> had   figure   together   talking   stopped   out   seeing

4. 退出する前にテスト用紙を提出してください。よい休暇をお過ごしください。

Please (_____) (_____) your test (   ) (   )

you (   ). Have a nice (   ).

> vacation   in   before   papers   give   leave   hand

● Discussion Questions

1. What activities would be safe in face-to-face English classes taught during a pandemic?

2. What possible problems could occur in online classes at colleges? Why?

Students Keeping Memory of Shuri Castle Alive

首里城を語り継ぐ高校生たち

首里城の火災により、正殿等の重要な建造物が焼失した。沖縄の人々に与えた衝撃ははかり知れない。「興南アクト部」である中学生と高校生のメンバーたちは、それでも現地のガイド活動にこだわり、修学旅行生たちに城の歴史や文化の説明をしている。交流と貢献がモットーである彼らの前向きな活動と努力に密着リポートする。

STUDENTS KEEPING MEMORY OF SHURI CASTLE ALIVE

● Words & Phrases

CD 04

- [ ] **aftermath** （事故、災害などの）結果、余波
- [ ] **iconic** 象徴的な、伝統的形式による
- [ ] to **take ... in** 〜を理解する
- [ ] to **press on** 頑張って進める

  The craftsman tirelessly *pressed on* with his work.

  その職人は根気強く自分の仕事を続けた。

- [ ] to **convene** 《正式》（会など）を招集する
- [ ] **loved one** 最愛の人、恋人
- [ ] to **settle on** 〜を決定する、選ぶ
- [ ] **goggles** ゴーグル
- [ ] **circumstance** 《通例、複数形》事情、状況〈cf. circum-（まわりに）＋ -stance（立っていること）〉

  It all depends on the *circumstances*.

  それはすべて状況によります。

- [ ] **affection** 愛情
- [ ] **resourcefulness** 臨機応変、機転
- [ ] **firsthand** 直接

以下は、浅草の観光案内です。下の枠内から適切な単語を選び、空所に入れましょう。

1. 浅草は東京の繁華街で、観光客向けのみやげ店が多くあります。日本で最も人気のある観光（目的）地の一つです。

Asakusa is a (　　　　　　　　　　) area, which has a lot of (　　　　　　　　) shops for tourists. It is one of the most popular tourist (　　　　　　　　) in Japan.

2. 最初の浅草寺は 7 世紀に建立され、東京最古のお寺です。

The first Senso-ji Temple was (　　　　　　　　　　) in the 7th century and is the oldest temple in Tokyo.

3. 雷門は浅草寺に導く大きな朱塗りの門です。その門には大きな提灯と風神・雷神の一対の像があります。

Kaminarimon is a large vermilion gate which (　　　　　　　　　) to Senso-ji Temple. The gate has a huge (　　　　　　　　) and a pair of statues of gods, the wind god and thunder god.

4. 本堂は本尊の観音様を祀（まつ）っています。

The main hall (　　　　　　　　) the statue of Kannon, the (　　　　　　　　) of Mercy.

5. 浅草花やしきは 19 世紀半ばに開園された日本で最初の遊園地です。

Asakusa Hanayashiki opened in the (　　　　　　　　) of the 19th century and was the first (　　　　　　　　) park in Japan.

amusement	constructed	destinations	downtown
enshrines	Goddess	lantern	leads　　middle　　souvenir

Watch the News　　　　　　　　　　**First Viewing**

ニュースを見て、内容と合っているものは T、違っているものは F を選びましょう。

1. This was the first year that the school club held guided tours for tourists.　　[T / F]

2. It was discovered that the fire occurred because someone had been smoking in the castle.

[T / F]

3. The first guided tour the club held after the fire turned out well.　　[T / F]

1 ニュースをもう一度見て、各問の空所に入る適切な選択肢を a〜c から選びましょう。

1. After they learned about the fire, the club members
had ____ to prepare for the next guided tour.
a. only two weeks
b. just one month
c. under three months

2. The club members decided to use ____ for the tour.
a. only old pictures taken before the fire
b. VR goggles and photos of Shuri Castle
c. paintings and newspaper articles

3. After the fire, the volunteer members of the club
guided ____.
a. 130 students from neighboring cities in Okinawa
b. fewer than 150 participants from central Japan
c. over 300 senior high school students from Shiga
Prefecture

2 以下の各情報を、ニュースに出てきた順序に並べましょう。

1. In the school, the students worked on redesigning their guided tour for visitors.
2. The castle gate was locked after the devastating fire so that no one could come in.
3. One tourist was impressed by the love the Okinawans have for the damaged castle.
4. The leader of the volunteer club said sadly that the castle site looks very different now.

3 CD の音声を聞いて、次ページ News Story の ❶〜❼ の文中にある空所に適切な単語
を書き入れましょう。音声は 2 回繰り返されます。　　　　　　　　　　◎ CD 05

Anchor: People in Okinawa are still dealing with the **aftermath** of a
    fire that destroyed Shuri Castle more than three months ago.
    For one group of students with a special relationship *for** the
    iconic landmark, the loss has left them with some tough
5   decisions.

Atsuki Nakamura (Konan Act Club leader): ❶ (¹)
    (²) (³) (⁴)
    (⁵) since the castle burned down. We are about
    to enter the grounds for the first time since the fire.

10 *Narrator:* For years this school club has been offering guided tours of
    the landmark to students from across Japan.

    After surveying the area, they were shocked by the extent of the
    damage.

Nakamura: It's really hard to **take** this **in**. ❷ It (¹)
15   (²) (³) (⁴)
    (⁵) (⁶) (⁷) we've
    come to know so well through our tours.

Narrator: The site has played an important role in Okinawan culture
    for 500 years, but disaster struck one night in October.
20   Investigators say an electrical problem may be to blame. Now
    the group has to decide whether to **press on**. Their next tour is
    just two months away, so they **convene** a meeting to discuss
    what to do.

Nakamura: It's not the Shuri Castle we know. ❸ I think students
25   coming on a field trip will (¹) (²)
    (³) (⁴) (⁵)
    (⁶) (⁷).

Marina Shingaki: It's like we've lost a **loved one**. I want to tell the
    students who come here that that's how we Okinawans feel.

❶ その門は閉ざ
   されていた

❷ 〜の場所だと
   は全く思えな
   い[見えない]

❸ これは大変な
   損失だという
   ことを理解す
   る

Narrator: Next comes the hard part, how to bring the castle back to life for visitors. They **settle on** using photos and virtual reality **goggles** and spend the coming weeks redesigning the tour.

At last, the big day arrives. The participants are 130 students from Shiga Prefecture on Japan's main island.

Kasumi Okura *(Konan Act Club deputy leader):* We have been giving tours of Shuri Castle, a symbol of Okinawa, for years. ❹ Even though it has burned down, I (¹) (²) (³) (⁴) (⁵) (⁶).

❹ 皆さんの訪問
をお楽しみい
ただきたいと
思います

Narrator: ❺ Despite the **circumstances**, the club members do their best (¹) (²) (³) (⁴) (⁵) and to keep the memory of the castle alive.

❺ 友好的な雰囲
気を作り出す
のに

Student 1: It was easy to understand. I enjoyed it.

Student 2: I was very impressed with how much **affection** they have for this lost treasure.

Narrator: Thanks to the dedication and **resourcefulness** of the club members, their first tour since the fire was a success.

Nakamura: ❻ This was an opportunity to show (¹) (²) (³) (⁴) (⁵) (⁶) and pass our mission down to our younger members.

❻ 僕たちはまだ
こうした行事
が開催できる

Narrator: ❼ The road to rebuilding Shuri Castle will be long, but the club is ensuring students across Japan still have (¹) (²) (³) (⁴) (⁵) (⁶) (⁷) **firsthand**.

❼ その文化財に
ついて学ぶ機
会

Note
＊ with が正しい

Review the Key Expressions

各問、選択肢から適切な単語を選び、英文を完成させましょう。なお、余分な単語が1語ずつあります。

1. 営業部の人たちは客のクレーム<u>を</u>効果的に<u>処理する</u>ように、訓練を受けている。

(　　　　　　) people in the (　　　　　　) department are (　　　　　　) to (　　　　　　) effectively (　　　　　　) customer (　　　　　　).

| with | in | those | complaints | trained | sales | deal |

2. 私が<u>やろうとしている</u>時に、なんでいつもやりなさいって言うの。

(　　　　　　) do you always tell me (　　　　　　) to (　　　　　　) just (　　　　　　) I'm (　　　　　　) (　　　　　　) do it?

| to | what | do | how | about | why | when |

3. 国際的なフェスティバルの参加者を楽しませておくのに、音楽は重要な<u>役目を果たす</u>。

Music (　　　　　　) an (　　　　　　) (　　　　　　) in (　　　　　　) the (　　　　　　) of our international festival (　　　　　　).

| happy | important | keeping | plays | role | participants | playing |

4. Zoom <u>のおかげで</u>、国際会議を開いて外国にいる友だちと連絡を取っておくことが簡単にできる。

(　　　　　　) (　　　　　　) Zoom, it's easy to hold international (　　　　　　) and (　　　　　　) in (　　　　　　) with (　　　　　　) in other countries.

| friends | to | conferences | according | touch | keep | thanks |

● Discussion Questions

1. What's the most memorable trip you have ever taken? What do you remember most about it?

2. What club activities have you participated in? Which did you enjoy and why?

UNIT 3

A Bitter Taste for Healthy Fish

魚が食べないレジ袋

プラスチックは耐久性に富み安価に生産できることから、レジ袋や建設資材など用途も幅広い。しかし利用後きちんと処理されず、海洋プラスチックが世界的な環境問題になってきた。プラスチックを誤って食べてしまう海洋動物を救うにはどうするか。ある高校生のグループが魚が食べないレジ袋を考案した。

HIGH SCHOOL SCIENTISTS FIND WAY TO PROTECT FISH

● Words & Phrases

CD 06

☐ **bait** （釣り針・わなにつける）えさ、餌

☐ to **spit out** 〜を吐き出す

The food tasted so terrible that he had to *spit* it *out*.

その食べ物はあまりにもひどい味がしたので、彼はしかたなく吐き出した。

☐ **ingredient** （混合物の）成分、原料

☐ to **ingest** （食物など）を摂取する、飲み込む

☐ to **come up with** 〜を思いつく

The inventor *came up with* an ingenious idea.

その発明家は独創的な考えを思いついた。

☐ to **throw away** 〜を捨てる

☐ **substance** 物質、物

☐ **denatonium** デナトニウム〈安息香酸デナトニウムは少量で強い苦味があり、誤飲防止の添加物として利用される〉

☐ to **devise** 〜を考案する

☐ **biodegradable** 生物分解性の

☐ to **decompose** 分解する

☐ **inhabitant** 生息動物

以下は、環境問題に関する記述です。下の枠内から適切な単語を選び、空所に入れましょう。

1. 地球環境問題は緊急の対処を要する。
   Global ( ) problems need our ( ) attention.

2. その企業は環境に優しい商品を生産している。
   The company produces environmentally ( ) products.

3. 温室効果ガス排出を削減するため、みんなもっと頻繁に公共交通機関を使うべきだ。
   People should use public transportation more often to reduce ( ) gas ( ).

4. 可燃ゴミは不燃物と注意深く分別されるべきだ。
   ( ) waste should be carefully separated from ( ).

5. 私たちはより明るい未来のため、持続可能な生活スタイルに従わなければならない。
   We must follow a ( ) lifestyle for a brighter future.

6. 二酸化炭素の排出量増加が、温暖化を強めている。
   The increase of carbon ( ) emissions is boosting global ( ).

7. オゾン層が、大気に入ってくる紫外線の強さを抑えることができる。
   The ozone layer can reduce the intensity of ( ) rays entering our atmosphere.

burnable	dioxide	emissions	environmental	friendly
greenhouse	sustainable	ultraviolet	unburnable	urgent	warming

ニュースを見て、内容と合っているものは T、違っているものは F を選びましょう。

1. Watanabe invented grocery bags which tastes sour to fish.　　　　[T / F]

2. The students' project won recognition in a business contest.　　　　[T / F]

3. To produce their design, the students are collaborating with a company.　　[T / F]

1 ニュースをもう一度見て、各問の空所に入る適切な選択肢を a 〜 c から選びましょう。

1. Every year, ＿＿ tons of plastic garbage is thrown into
seas around the world.

  a. eighty thousand

  b. millions of

  c. eight billion

2. Denatonium is a material which ＿＿.

  a. can dissolve plastics

  b. doesn't taste good to fish

  c. is designed to clean water

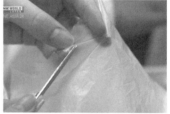

3. Of the plastic waste in the ocean, ＿＿.

  a. little of it is grocery bags

  b. half of it is plastic bottles

  c. the majority of it is biodegradable

2 右の文字列を並べ替えて単語を作り、各文の空所に入れて意味がとおるようにしましょう。一部の文字が与えてあるものもあります。

1. The fish spat out the plastic pieces in the (**ex**＿＿＿).　　　　[meritpen]

2. The fish in the tank snapped at the (＿＿＿) .　　　　[tiba]

3. A lot of garbage (＿＿ **ed**) up on the shore.　　　　[whas]

4. These grocery bags taste terrible, but are not (**poi**＿＿) for animals. [usonso]

3 CD の音声を聞いて、次ページ News Story の❶〜❼の文中にある空所に適切な単語を書き入れましょう。音声は 2 回繰り返されます。　　　　◎ CD 07

Anchor: Eight million tons of plastic garbage is thought to end up in the world's oceans every year. ❶ When fish eat it, (¹) (²) (³) (⁴) (⁵). ❷ Some high school students in Japan have found (¹) (²) (³) (⁴) (⁵) (⁶) and protect the animals.

❶ 結果は致命的
になりうる

❷ その過程を防
ぐ方法

Narrator: The group is about to find out if its idea works.

Student : Let's start the experiment.

Narrator: ❸ The students (¹) (²) (³) (⁴) (⁵) (⁶) small pieces. They then *mix** the pieces into **bait** and gave it to their fish. The fish ate the bait but **spat out** the plastic pieces.

❸ プラスチック
のレジ袋を〜
にする

Student: Hey, they're spitting it out.

Narrator: The students had worked out a test to see if mixing **ingredients** that fish don't like into plastic bags would prevent the fish from **ingesting** them.

Watanabe Kokomi **came up with** the concept of trying it with grocery bags. She noticed trash washed up on the beach and wanted to do something about it.

Watanabe Kokomi: ❹ We can (¹) (²) (³) (⁴) (⁵) (⁶) that gets **thrown away** but not all of it, so I came up with the idea of making grocery bags that fish dislike.

❹ ごみを拾う

Narrator: Watanabe's team learned about a **substance** called **denatonium**. ❺ Toy makers often use it to (¹) (²) (³) (⁴) (⁵) (⁶) they shouldn't. It's bitter

❺ 子供たちが不
意に何か〜の
ものを食べる
のを防ぐ

but not poisonous.

With university assistance, the high school scientists were able to **devise** the experiment. They found that most fish would spit out the plastic when four percent of the mixture was denatonium. The project won second prize in a high school business contest.

The students are now working with a company to turn their design into a product. For a greater effect, they're combining the denatonium with **biodegradable** materials. ❻ In that way, the bags will **decompose** in the ocean (¹)
(²) (³) (⁴)
(⁵).

❻ 数年以内で

Watanabe: We really need to show our project to people who keep throwing out plastic garbage. ❼ (¹)
(²) (³) (⁴)
(⁵) (⁶) that you can begin with something this simple.

❼ 彼らに知って
　 ほしい

Narrator: Grocery bags only account for a small portion of plastic waste. But they're a place to start in keeping the ocean and its **inhabitants** healthy.

Note
＊ 前後の動詞の時制に合わせて mixed としたほうがよい。

Review the Key Expressions

各問、選択肢から適切な単語を選び、英文を完成させましょう。なお、余分な単語が1語ずつあります。

1. そのシンガーソングライターは、海辺を歩いている時にその曲を思いついたと言った。

The singer-songwriter said that he (＿＿＿＿＿＿) (＿＿＿＿＿＿) (＿＿＿＿＿＿)

the song (＿＿＿＿) he was (＿＿＿＿) on the (＿＿＿＿).

beach　came　when　with　down　walking　up

2. 生ゴミを捨てないで。その代わり、庭の土を肥沃にするのに使うべきです。

Don't (＿＿＿＿＿＿) garbage (＿＿＿＿＿＿)! (＿＿＿＿＿＿), you

(＿＿＿＿＿＿) use it to (＿＿＿＿＿＿) the (＿＿＿＿＿＿) in your garden.

should　away　enrich　instead　get　soil　throw

3. その会社の社長は長年一生懸命働き、自分の小さな事業を 10 億ドル企業に変えることができた。

The company (＿＿＿＿＿＿) worked very hard for (＿＿＿＿＿＿) years and

successfully (＿＿＿＿＿＿) his small business (＿＿＿＿＿＿) a

(＿＿＿＿＿＿)-dollar (＿＿＿＿＿＿).

into　enterprise　million　president　turned　billion　many

4. 最近、留学生の数が増加し、（今では）この大学の学生数の一割を占めている。

The number of (＿＿＿＿＿＿) students (＿＿＿＿＿＿) increased recently, and they

(＿＿＿＿＿＿) (＿＿＿＿＿＿) over (＿＿＿＿＿＿) percent of our college

(＿＿＿＿＿＿).

has　population　one　international　ten　for　account

● Discussion Questions

1. Do you think it's good for customers to be charged for grocery bags? Why?

2. How many categories of trash do you sort in your city: e.g., burnable, recyclable? Is this system good? Why?

Robots Luring Diners Back

ロボット販売のハンバーガー？

モスフードサービスは分身ロボットを活用した「ゆっくりレジ」を稼働させた。会話を楽しみながら商品を選択する人向けに企画され、ロボットは身体障がいなどの社会的ハンディキャップで外出の困難な人が担当し、注文時の応対を可能にしている。今後は更なる応用などを視野に入れた事業の展開が期待されている。

ROBOTS LURING DINERS BACK TO RESTAURANTS

● Words & Phrases

CD 08

☐ **coronavirus** 新型コロナウイルス〈cf. 病気の正式名 COVID-19 は Corona, Virus, Disease, 2019 年を組み合わせた造語〉

☐ **pandemic** 世界的流行病

☐ **twofold** 二要素のある、二重の

☐ **vulnerable** 攻撃されやすい

☐ **custom-made** 特注の、オーダーメイドの〈cf. 反意語は、ready-made 既製品の〉

☐ to **staff** [stæf] ～にスタッフを配置する〈cf. stuff [stʌf] の意味は「もの」。発音の違いにも注意〉

☐ to **cut down on** ～を削減する

☐ to **keep ... at bay** ～を寄せ付けない、食い止める
The alarm system *keeps* robbers *at bay*.
アラームシステムが強盗を寄せ付けない。

☐ **customer interaction** 接客

☐ **start-up** 新興企業

☐ **further** （程度などが）さらに進んだ、それ以上の
If you have *further* questions, feel free to contact us.
さらにご質問があれば、お気軽にお問い合わせ下さい。

以下は、ファストフード店でよく使う表現です。下の枠内から適切な単語を選び、空所に入れましょう。

1. こんにちは。ご注文をどうぞ［何をご注文でしょうか］。
   Hello. What (   ) you like to order?

2. こちらでお召し上がりですか、それともお持ち帰りですか。
   For (   ), or to (   )?

3. このセットメニューはハンバーガー、お飲み物のS、それにフライドポテトのSになります。
   This (   ) includes a hamburger, a small drink and a small order of
   (   ) fries.

4. ダブルチーズバーガーとコーラのMをお願いします。
   A double cheese burger and a (   ) Coke, please.

5. フィレオフィッシュバーガーとチョコレートシェークのLをください。
   I'll take a fillet-o'-fish burger and a large chocolate (   ).

6. ポテトにケチャップ（の小袋）を1つ余分にいただけますか。
   Can I have an (   ) bag of ketchup with my fries?

7. この番号札をもって、テーブルでお待ちください。
   (   ) this number and (   ) at your table, please.

8. トレイはあちらの場所にお戻し下さい。
   Please (   ) back your tray to that section (   ) there.

9. 全部で9ドル50セントになります。
   That'll be nine (   ) and 50 cents, all together.

bring	combo	dollars	extra	French	go	here
medium	over	shake	take	wait	would	

ニュースを見て、内容と合っているものはT、違っているものはFを選びましょう。

1. Human staff workers are frequently not available at this fast food restaurant.　　[T / F]

2. The robot at the counter may give advice to customers about what they should order.

　　　　　　　　　　　　　　　　　　　　　　　　　　　　　　　　[T / F]

3. All staff members at the restaurant are disabled.　　　　　　　　[T / F]

1 ニュースをもう一度見て、各問の空所に入る適切な選択肢を a 〜 c から選びましょう。

1. The robot ____.

  a. is more than 20 centimeters tall

  b. weighs approximately 23 kilograms

  c. is placed at least 23 cm away from customers

2. A ____ manufactured this robot.

  a. well-established company

  b. newly established business

  c. famous inventor in Osaka

3. At a meeting held recently, the company decided to ____.

  a. start another restaurant chain in the Tokyo area

  b. add a new sensor to improve the robot's function

  c. design another type of robot for their drive-thru service

2 以下はニュースの概要です。空所に適切な単語を書き入れましょう。語頭の文字（群）
は与えてあります。

Restaurants cannot make much money because many people are (**s**   ¹) at
home due to this (**p**   ²) . The owner of a fast food restaurant chain came up
with a (**tw**   ³) solution, so customers can avoid being infected and disabled
people can be employed. Instead of human workers, this small (**r**   ⁴) takes
orders. Actually, people with (**d**   ⁵) provide its voice. Mr. Kasai, the
(**ex**   ⁶) of the burger chain, feels the human touch is important in interacting
with customers. The company that developed the robot is planning on further efforts for
better service.

3 CD の音声を聞いて、次ページ News Story の❶〜❼の文中にある空所に適切な単語
を書き入れましょう。音声は 2 回繰り返されます。　　　　　　　　　　　　◉ CD 09

Anchor: Now, many restaurant owners are feeling the pinch as people stay away amid the **coronavirus pandemic**. But as you'll see in this next story, one unique solution has a benefit that's **twofold**. ❶ Not only (　　　　¹⁾) (　　　　²⁾) (　　　　³⁾) (　　　　⁴⁾) (　　　　⁵⁾) (　　　　⁶⁾), it also gives opportunities to more **vulnerable** members of society.

5

Narrator: At this burger chain in Tokyo, customers are being served up an unexpected side of entertainment.

10 ***Man:*** (*He is at the order counter with his friend.*) What? Really?

Robot (Man's voice): Hello, welcome.

Narrator: This robot greets customers and takes orders, all while wearing a **custom-made** uniform for its 23-centimeter-tall frame.

15　Diners receive their meals at the cash register nearby which is **staffed** with a person. ❷ The system aims to (　　　　¹⁾) (　　　　²⁾) (　　　　³⁾) (　　　　⁴⁾) (　　　　⁵⁾) by **cutting down on** human contact. But taking orders isn't the robot's only important job.

20 ***Robot (Woman's voice):*** Hello.

Boys: Hello.

Robot: Did you choose your order yet?

Boys: No, not yet. Hmmm.

Boy1: I usually get the teriyaki burger.

25 ***Robot:*** Same as me! I like teriyaki burgers too. They're delicious, aren't they!

Boy1: Yup.

Narrator: It also helps customers decide what to eat.

❶ それが、食事客が安心する助けとなる

❷ 感染の危険を減らす

❸ This is because the robot is controlled by (1)

(2) (3) (4)

(5) (6).

Robot: Anything else with that order?

5 *Narrator:* The robot is allowing people with disabilities to work from anywhere, providing employment opportunities that are convenient as well as **keeping** the coronavirus **at bay**.

❹ Kasai Ko is the executive of the burger chain (1) (2) (3)

10 (4) (5). He felt it was important to keep a human touch in **customer interactions**.

Kasai Ko (Executive Officer, Mos Food Services): ❺ If we can provide good customer service while social distancing, (1) (2) (3)

15 (4) (5) (6)

(7) in the service sector.

Narrator: Here's the **start-up** in Tokyo that developed the robot.

❻ Customer feedback (1) (2)

(3) (4) (5)

20 (6) plan for **further** improvements. At a recent meeting, they decided to add a sensor to quickly alert the robot to a customer's arrival, in response to the restaurant's requests for prompt service.

Robot: Hello, welcome.

25 *Narrator:* ❼ The pandemic has not just (1)

(2) (3) (4)

(5) (6). Instead, it's creating opportunities to innovate that keep us connected.

---

❸ 遠隔で働いている実際の人たち

❹ ロボット（を活用した）企画を推進した

❺ それが多くの新しい可能性を開くだろう

❻ 彼らに～する機会を与えた

❼ 私たちの社会生活を制限した

Note

以上のサービスは 2020 年 9 月 25 日の番組放送時点の情報である。

Review the Key Expressions

各問、選択肢から適切な単語を選び、英文を完成させましょう。なお、余分な単語が1語ずつあります。

1. 私は今年の9月までに、TOEIC®L&Rテストで800点以上とることを目標にしています。

I am (　　　　　　　) (　　　　　　　) get (　　　　　　　) (　　　　　　　) 800

(　　　　　　　) the TOEIC® L&R TEST (　　　　　　　) September of this year.

by　aiming　more　during　to　on　than

2. その女の子は甘いものを減らし、もっと運動することで7キロ減量した。

The girl (　　　　　　　) seven (　　　　　　　) by (　　　　　　　)

(　　　　　　　) (　　　　　　　) sweets and (　　　　　　　) more.

up　exercising　kilos　down　cutting　on　lost

3. アメリカの国会議事堂のまわりのガードたちは、抗議者たちを近づけないようにそこに在駐している。

The (　　　　　　　) (　　　　　　　) the U.S. Capitol building (　　　　　　　)

there to (　　　　　　　) protesters (　　　　　　　) (　　　　　　　) .

around　at　guards　wall　keep　bay　are

4. その若者はあまり真剣に働かない。その代わりいつも時間を浪費し、不注意な間違いばかりする。

The (　　　　　　　) man doesn't take his (　　　　　　　) very (　　　　　　　) .

(　　　　　　　), he (　　　　　　　) time and (　　　　　　　) a lot of

(　　　　　　　) mistakes.

wastes　instead　young　careless　seriously　adult　work　makes

● Discussion Questions

1. Would you be interested in being served by a robot at your table in restaurants? Why?

2. More and more workers are being replaced by AI robots. Do you think this is a good idea? Why?

Toilet Designs Aim to Flush Away Issues

公共トイレ革命
—— 斬新なデザイン

渋谷区の公園に透明な公共トイレが現れた。日本財団の THE TOKYO TOILET プロジェクトの一環なのだが、かなりインパクトが強い。様々なタイプのトイレがあり、休息所を備えた公共空間を意識しているものもある。公共トイレの暗い、汚い、臭いといった、イメージを一掃し日本のもてなしの心を世界にアピールする。

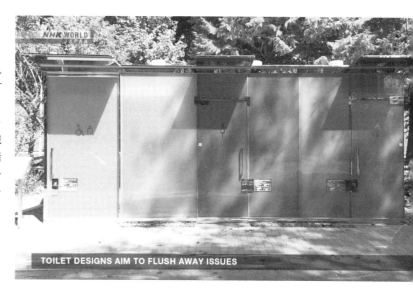

TOILET DESIGNS AIM TO FLUSH AWAY ISSUES

● Words & Phrases

CD 10

☐ to **pop up**　突然現れる

A website advertising a new electronic musical instrument just *popped up*.

新しい電子楽器を宣伝するウェブサイトができた。

☐ to **flush away**　きれいに洗い流す

☐ **misconception**　誤解、思い違い

☐ **fuss**　騒ぎ

☐ **squid-shaped**　イカの形をした

☐ **buzz**　《口語》話題、噂〈多くの人々があることについて話し、ざわついているイメージ〉

☐ **stall**　仕切った小室

☐ **call of nature**　自然の欲求〈トイレに行くこと〉

☐ **transparent**　透明な

☐ **cheeky**　《俗語》ずうずうしい、大胆不敵な〈イギリス英語〉

☐ to **convey**　〜を伝える、運ぶ

Words alone cannot *convey* my true feelings.

私の本当の気持ちはことばだけでは伝えられない。

Before You Watch

以下はトイレ等に関する表現です。下の枠内から適切なものを選び、空所に入れましょう。

1. 【よく知らない人と会話中に】「ちょっと失礼します。すぐに戻ってきます。」
Please excuse me. I'll be right (   ).

2. 【友人に】「ちょっと待ってて、トイレに行ってきます。」
Wait a (   ). I've got to go to the (   ).

3. 【友人の家で】「トイレお借りしてもいいですか。」
Can I (   ) your bathroom?

4. **レストラン客**「すみません、トイレはどこですか。」
店員「まっすぐ行って右に曲がれば、左手にあります。」
Customer: Excuse me, (   ) is the restroom/bathroom?
Server: Go (   ) and (   ) right. It's on your
(   ).

5. **A**「お手洗いに行きたいんだけど。」
B「がまんして。もうすぐ着くから。」
A: I really need to go to the bathroom.
B: Can you (   )? We're (   ) there.

6. トイレが詰まった。
The toilet is (   ).

7. シンクの水が流れない。
The sink won't (   ).

almost	back	bathroom	drain	hold it	left
minute	plugged up	straight	turn	use	where

Watch the News　　　　　　　　　　　　　**First Viewing**

ニュースを見て、内容と合っているものは T、違っているものは F を選びましょう。

1. The restroom walls cloud up after you lock the door. [T / F]

2. This clear glass public toilet was designed by a famous architect, Ban Shigeru. [T / F]

3. Seven toilets were replaced with no more planned for replacement. [T / F]

Understand the News Second Viewing

1 ニュースをもう一度見て、各問の空所に入る適切な選択肢を a 〜 c から選びましょう。

1. According to an architect, people worry that ____.
   a. it may smell bad in the toilet
   b. the public toilet may be closed
   c. someone might be hiding inside the toilet

2. The public toilet by Ando Tadao ____.
   a. allows fresh air flow through the facilities
   b. is much bigger than other public toilets
   c. is often designed in the shape of an octopus

3. The Nippon Foundation says that their project ____.
   a. mainly focuses on larger sized public toilets
   b. should change people's attitude towards public toilets
   c. will be extended to other metropolitan areas

2 以下はニュースの概要です。空所に適切な単語を書き入れましょう。語頭の文字（群）
は与えてあります。

Eye-catching (**p**   [1]) toilets are being built in some parks in Tokyo. One of these structures is drawing special (**at**   [2]). It is surrounded by colorful ([3]). You can see everything that's inside. When you lock the door from inside, the (**tr**   [4]) glass becomes frosted. Ban Shigeru, an (**a**   [5])-winning architect, came up with this unique idea. Other top architects also designed ingenious shapes and structures based on their own concepts. There are ten more toilets on the (**w**   [6]) for use in Tokyo.

3 CD の音声を聞いて、次ページ News Story の❶〜❼の文中にある空所に適切な単語
を書き入れましょう。音声は 2 回繰り返されます。　　　　　　　　　　◎ CD 11

Anchor: ❶ Well, some (¹⁾ (²⁾

(³⁾ (⁴⁾ (⁵⁾

(⁶⁾ here in Tokyo. The simple Instagram-worthy

designs are part of a plan to flush away **misconceptions** about

public toilets. NHK World's Yamamoto Saori went to see what

all the **fuss** is about.

Narrator: (*Different types of public toilets are shown.*) A striking red

building inspired by traditional wrapping techniques. A **squid-

shaped** design that looks at home in a popular park.

Each one came from the mind of a top Japanese architect. They

are all creating a **buzz**, but these colorful, transformed **stalls** are

drawing the most attention, even among people who don't hear

the **call of nature**.

Reporter (Yamamoto Saori): ❷ It may seem risky to use these toilets,

but step inside, close the door, lock it, and (¹⁾

(²⁾ (³⁾ (⁴⁾

(⁵⁾ (⁶⁾.

Narrator: ❸ This smart glass is only **transparent** when electrical

current is running through it, so you won't be caught with your

p a n t s   d o w n, (¹⁾ (²⁾

(³⁾ (⁴⁾ (⁵⁾

(⁶⁾.

Ban Shigeru came up with the **cheeky** idea. The award-winning

architect is known around the world for his innovative designs.

The impressive buildings aren't just made to look nice. ❹ Each

h a s   s o m e   s p e c i a l   m e a n i n g,   a n d (¹⁾

(²⁾ (³⁾ (⁴⁾

(⁵⁾ (⁶⁾.

Ban Shigeru (Architect): Before they go in, people worry that the

toilets aren't clean or that someone could be hiding inside.

❶ かなり目を引
く建築物が出
現している

❷ 必要なプライ
バシーが得ら
れる

❸ 電源が切れた
ら

❹ この最新作も
例外ではない

28

❺ I wanted to use design to (　　　　　¹)
(　　　　　²) (　　　　　³) (　　　　　⁴)
(　　　　　⁵) (　　　　　⁶) (　　　　　⁷).

❺ 多くの公共トイレが抱えている問題を解決する

Narrator: Addressing issues with public restrooms is what unites the project's facilities.

Ando Tadao is also a world-famous architect. He focused on making his design easy to access, with a unique shape and a structure that allows fresh air to flow through.

Ando Tadao (Architect) : I was inspired by the architects involved and wanted to do my best. The building's value isn't determined by its scale. This public toilet may be small, but it **conveys** an important message.

Narrator: So far, seven of these toilets have been installed in downtown Tokyo with ten more on the way. The nonprofit Nippon Foundation says it wants the project to change habits and minds.

Hanaoka Hayato (Project organizer): **❻** These unique and advanced designs make the toilets accessible for everyone, (　　　　　¹) (　　　　　²) (　　　　　³), (　　　　　⁴), (　　　　　⁵) (　　　　　⁶). Ultimately, it demonstrates the possibilities of an inclusive society.

❻ 性別、年齢、あるいは障がいのあるなしにかかわらず

Narrator: **❼** Everyone involved hopes this effort to elevate the humble public toilet won't end here, but instead (　　　　　¹) (　　　　　²) (　　　　　³) (　　　　　⁴) (　　　　　⁵) (　　　　　⁶).
Yamamoto Saori, NHK World.

❼ 世界中に、より良いデザインを啓発する

Review the Key Expressions

各問、選択肢から適切な単語を選び、英文を完成させましょう。なお、余分な単語が1語ずつあります。

1. 新宿駅の外のストリートシンガーが、魅惑的なハーモニーで多くの注意を引いた。

The street singers (　　　　　　　　) of Shinjuku Station (＿＿＿＿＿＿＿) a
(　　　　　　　) of (＿＿＿＿＿＿＿) with (　　　　　　) (　　　　　　　　)
harmony.

> their　outside　lot　beautiful　attention　loud　drew

2. 今日の授業では、ラテン語語源の新しい単語の意味の覚え方に焦点を当てます。

For today's lesson, we will (＿＿＿＿＿＿＿) (＿＿＿＿＿＿＿) (　　　　　　) the
(　　　　　　　) of new words (　　　　　) Latin (　　　　　　　).

> with　on　learning　origins　meanings　focus　memorize

3. いつかマスターズで戦えるように、全力を尽くしてゴルフのプレーの仕方を学びます。

I'll (＿＿＿＿＿＿) (＿＿＿＿＿＿) (＿＿＿＿＿＿) to learn (　　　　　) to
play golf (　　　　　) that I can (　　　　　　) in the Masters (　　　　　)
day.

> best　do　one　hold　how　so　compete　my

4. この頃暖かくなってきて梅の花が咲きそうだ。春はもうすぐだ。

It's getting warmer, and the (　　　　　　) trees are (　　　　　　) to
(　　　　　　). Spring is (＿＿＿＿＿＿) (＿＿＿＿＿＿) (＿＿＿＿＿＿).

> way　on　plum　flower　about　the　bloom

● Discussion Questions

1. Would you use transparent public toilets? What are their advantages and disadvantages?

2. In foreign countries you may have to pay for using public toilets. What do you think of this system? Why?

Teleworking Encourages Tokyo Exodus

テレワークで故郷へ

ここ数年サラリーマンにリモートワークが浸透してきた。また蔓延する伝染病を避ける意図もあって、都市圏を離れ移住先で新しい生活をする人が増加している。このリポートでは東京の勤務先を辞めずに東京脱出を果たした例を紹介する。地方に住みながら遠隔での仕事に軸足を置いて、同時に家族との豊かな生活も楽しんでいる。

TELEWORKING ENCOURAGES TOKYO EXODUS

● Words & Phrases

CD 12

□ **exodus**　集団移動、（大勢の人の）脱出

The tsunami warning caused a mass *exodus* of people from the coast.

津波警報で多くの人が海岸から避難した［移動した］。

□ **onset**　始まり

□ **peace and quiet**　平安と静寂、安らぎと静けさ

彼らは安らぎと静かな暮らしを求めて地方の別荘に行く。

They go to their cottage in the country for *peace and quiet*.

□ to **head**　〜へ向かう

□ **colleague**　同僚、仲間

□ **culture**　（会社の）社風

□ to **spread out**　（人々を）分散させる

□ **routine**　決まりきった仕事〈cf. 旅なれた道、route 道＋ -ine 手順が原義〉

□ to **prioritize**　〜を優先する

The company *prioritized* the safety of its employees.

その企業は社員の安全を優先した。

Before You Watch

以下は、テレワークや生活スタイルに関する表現です。下の枠内から適切な単語を選び、空所に入れましょう。

1. 明日は在宅勤務をします。　I'm going to work from (　　　　　　　　) tomorrow.

2. うちの会社はテレワークを許可しています。
Our company allows us to work (　　　　　　　　).

3. ほとんどの同僚は、いま週に数回在宅勤務をしています。
Most of my (　　　　　　　) are (　　　　　　　　) now a few days a week.

4. インターネット接続が不安定で仕事になりません。
I can't get my work (　　　　　　　) with this unstable internet (　　　　　　　　).

5. 企業が休業している間、わたしたちが経済を回すのは可能ですか。
Is it possible to keep the economy (　　　　　　　　) while businesses are (　　　　　　　) down?

6. 公共交通機関を利用するとき、本当に社会的距離が維持できますか。
Can we really maintain (　　　　　　　　) distancing when we take public (　　　　　　　) ?

7. みんな頻繁に石鹸で手を洗って、咳エチケットを実践すべきです。
People should wash their hands frequently with soap and (　　　　　　　) good (　　　　　　　) etiquette.

8. 新型コロナの検査を受けて陰性でした。
I got (　　　　　　　) for COVID-19 and the result was (　　　　　　　　).

colleagues	connection	cough	done	going
home	negative	practice	remotely	shut
social	teleworking	tested	transportation	

Watch the News   First Viewing

ニュースを見て、内容と合っているものは T 、違っているものは F を選びましょう。

1. Sato moved back to his hometown five years ago.　　　　　　[T / F]

2. Sato works for an IT company and communicates with his clients online.　　[T / F]

3. When Sato worked in Tokyo, he frequently ate meals at home.　　[T / F]

1 ニュースをもう一度見て、各問の空所に入る適切な選択肢を a 〜 c から選びましょう。

1. ____ of the whole Japanese population lives in the Greater Tokyo area.

   a. About three percent

   b. Less than one third

   c. Approximately one half

2. Sato's current office is located ____ away from Tokyo.

   a. only five minutes

   b. around 33 km

   c. over 300 km

3. Sato is planning to ____.

   a. move back to Tokyo in a few years

   b. take over his father's farm next year

   c. keep living in Yamagata Prefecture

2 右の文字列を並べ替えて単語を作り、各文の空所に入れて意味がとおるようにしましょう。語頭の文字（群）は与えてあります。

1. A (**p**　　　　　　　) is a huge number of cases of a dangerous disease happening all over the world.　　　　　　　　　　　　　　　　　　　[icnmdea]

2. Sato loves the (**p**　　　　　　) and quiet of his hometown.　　　[ceae]

3. Sato helps his father with his (**fa**　　　　　　) in Yamagata.　　[mrokrw]

4. Sato's (**wo**　　　　　) is his parents' house.　　　　　　　　[cerkapl]

3 CD の音声を聞いて、次ページ News Story の❶〜❼の文中にある空所に適切な単語を書き入れましょう。音声は 2 回繰り返されます。　　　　　　　　　◎ CD 13

Anchor: ...and about 30 percent of Japan's total population live in the Greater Tokyo area, the capital and surrounding prefectures. But since the **onset** of the coronavirus pandemic, a growing number of people have been switching to remote work from the

5 **peace and quiet** of their hometowns out in the countryside. We look at one man who made that move three years ago.

Narrator: ❶ Sato Yoshihisa is a (¹) (²) (³) (⁴) (⁵) (⁶) (⁷), but he lives in Yamagata

10 Prefecture, about 330 kilometers away. He's **heading** to his office inside his parents' house, just five-minutes' walk from his home.

❶ 東京にある
IT 会社のコ
ンサルタント

Sato Yoshihisa (IT consultant) : (*To parents*) Good morning. (*To the reporter*) This is my workplace.

15 **Narrator:** Sato develops IT systems for companies. ❷ In 2017 he decided to (¹) (²) (³) (⁴) (⁵) (⁶) (⁷). Now he does all his work remotely.

❷ 東京を出て故
郷に戻る

20 As a rule, all his meetings with **colleagues** and clients are done online. They also like to chat online during breaks in their work.

(*Sato talks online with his colleagues.*)

Colleague: ❸ We (¹) (²)

25 (³) (⁴) (⁵) (⁶) (⁷) while we were working. I'm glad we've kept that same **culture**.

❸ いつも職場で
おしゃべりし
ていた

Sato Y.: ❹ We're all **spread out** now, so it's important to keep in touch individually (¹) (²) (³) (⁴) (⁵) (⁶)*.

❹ 後輩の社員の
ひとり一人と

5 **Narrator:** ❺ (¹) (²) (³) (⁴) (⁵) (⁶) (⁷), Sato heads home.

❺ 自分の仕事が
終わるとすぐ
に

Sato Y.: I'm home.

Kids: Welcome back!

10 **Narrator:** When he was working in Tokyo, he rarely had a chance to have dinner with his family on weekdays. ❻ After dinner, (¹) (²) (³) (⁴) (⁵) (⁶).

❻ 彼は赤ちゃん
をお風呂に入
れる

Sato Y.: This is my evening **routine**.

15 **Wife:** It's a big help. It gives me more time to put the other children to bed.

Narrator: On his days off, Sato helps his father with his farmwork.

Reporter: Are you happy that your son is back home?

Sato Kimiyoshi *(Father)*: Of course, I'm happy.

20 **Sato Y.:** It's great to be here in the place I like best. ❼ It's an opportunity to (¹) (²) (³) (⁴) (⁵) (⁶).

❼ 自分の故郷を
もっとよく知
るようになる

Reporter: Could you go back to living in the city?

25 **Sato Y.:** Well, I probably could go back, but I don't want to.

Narrator: More than a few people in Tokyo tend to **prioritize** their work, but a growing number are following Sato's example and moving back to their hometowns, far from the city but close to their families.

Note

＊(5)(6) に入る語彙は younger employees のほうがしぜんな言い方

Review the Key Expressions

各問、選択肢から適切な単語を選び、英文を完成させましょう。なお、余分な単語が 1 語ずつあります。

1. 定期的にフィットネスクラブで運動を始める前は、私は健康じゃなかった [不健康だった]。

I (＿＿＿＿＿＿) (＿＿＿＿＿＿) be (＿＿＿＿＿) of (＿＿＿＿＿) before I
started (＿＿＿＿) (＿＿＿＿＿) at the fitness club regularly.

| out | used | working | to | shape | out | in |

2. 佳純は前からの友だちと付き合いを続けるため、自分の地元に時々出かける。

Kasumi (＿＿＿＿＿) her hometown (＿＿＿＿＿) time (＿＿＿＿＿) time
to (＿＿＿＿＿) in (＿＿＿＿＿) (＿＿＿＿＿＿) her old friends.

| to | out | keep | from | touch | with | visits |

3. ステファニーは風邪をうつされるのが心配で、帰宅するとすぐに手を洗いうがいをする。

Stephanie is so (＿＿＿＿＿) about (＿＿＿＿＿) colds that (＿＿＿＿＿＿)
(＿＿＿＿＿＿) (＿＿＿＿＿) she gets home, she washes her hands and
(＿＿＿＿).

| soon | worried | as | catching | gargles | as | well |

4. 仕事がない日は、大輝には午前中ベッドから出る理由が [動機付け] がない。

On (＿＿＿＿＿＿) (＿＿＿＿＿) off, Daiki has no (＿＿＿＿＿) to
(＿＿＿＿) (＿＿＿＿) (＿＿＿＿＿) bed in the morning.

| in | out | his | get | days | of | motivation |

● Discussion Questions

1. Do you want to live and work in the metropolitan area? What kind of lifestyle do you expect to have?

2. What are some advantages and disadvantages of working online?

Learning to Love Rural Japan

秋田を学ぶ語学学校

秋田県小坂町の複合施設七滝活性化拠点センターに訪日外国人向けの AKITA INAKA SCHOOL が開校した。秋田の文化や田舎暮らしを体験しながら日本語を学ぶ。年齢・経歴もさまざまな第1期生が世界各地からやってきて8月のコースは好評のうちに行われた。言語・文化を通して交流の輪が広がった学びの日々を振り返る。

LEARNING TO LOVE RURAL JAPAN

● Words & Phrases

CD 14

- ☐ to **adapt**　順応する、適応する
- ☐ to **encourage**　人を〜するように励ます、仕向ける
- ☐ to **spread the word**　ニュースを広める
- ☐ to **interact with**　〜とふれ合う、交流する

　Sho *interacts* well *with* other students in class.
　翔はクラスの他の生徒たちとうまくやっている。

- ☐ **local**　地域住民、地元の人
- ☐ to **help oneself**　（食べ物を）自分で取って食べる

　Help yourself to another piece of cake.
　ケーキをもう一切れご自由にお取りください。

- ☐ **Bon Festival**　お盆
- ☐ **catalyst**　促進する働きをするもの
- ☐ to **revitalize**　〜を活性化する

Before You Watch

以下は、教室でよく使う表現です。下の枠内から適切な単語を選び、空所に入れましょう。

1. I'm going to take (　　　　　　　　) now.　今から出席をとります。

2. *Teacher:* Mike Brown?　マイク・ブラウン君（は、いますか）。
   Mike: (　　　　　　　　).　はい。

3. (　　　　　　　　) your textbook to page 46.　46 ページを開いてください。

4. Could you (　　　　　　　　) that again?　もう一度言ってくださいますか。

5. Can you (　　　　　　　　) me?　聞こえますか。

6. Any (　　　　　　　　)?　誰かやってみたい人は。

7. (　　　　　　　　) groups of four.　4 人のグループになってください。

8. Go back to your (　　　　　　　　).　自分の席に戻ってください。

9. (　　　　　　　　) your hand if you have any questions.
   質問があれば挙手してください。

10. (　　　　　　　　) everything, please.　全部片づけてください。

11. You (　　　　　　) a good (　　　　　　　　).　よくできました。

12. Let me give you this week's (　　　　　　　　).　今週の課題を出します。

13. It's (　　　　　　　　) next Tuesday.　締め切りは来週の火曜日です。

14. Oh! We've (　　　　　　　　) out of (　　　　　　　　).　時間が無くなりました。

15. Let's (　　　　　　　　) up today's class.　今日の授業は終わりです。

assignment	attendance	did	due	hear	here
job	make	put away	raise	run	say	seat
time	turn	volunteers	wrap		

Watch the News　　　　　　　　　　First Viewing

ニュースを見て、内容と合っているものは T、違っているものは F を選びましょう。

1. Matt wanted to learn both the Japanese language and about the local culture.　[T / F]

2. Heather says Kosaka is a lot quieter than San Francisco.　[T / F]

3. Michiko Fukui lives in the neighborhood of this school in Akita.　[T / F]

Understand the News

Second Viewing

1 ニュースをもう一度見て、各問の空所に入る適切な選択肢を a ～ c から選びましょう。

1. Some of these students are from ____.
   a. The U.K. and Mexico
   b. France and Italy
   c. India and Indonesia

2. The afternoon program includes ____.
   a. learning Japanese in class
   b. cooking Japanese dishes
   c. visiting other Japanese prefectures

3. Heather Brown originally came to Japan to ____.
   a. film a movie
   b. learn about kimono designs.
   c. join the Kanto Festival

2 ニュースに関して、空所に入る適切な数字を下の枠内から選びましょう。なお、余分な選択肢もあります。

1. There are (¹) international students in this school from all over the world.

2. These students are from (²) different countries and have various cultural backgrounds.

3. This school provides about (³) days of language classes and cultural experiences.

4. Heather Brown came to Japan (⁴) years ago because of her job.

4	6	8	10	12	14	20	24	30	32

3 CD の音声を聞いて、次ページ News Story の❶～❼の文中にある空所に適切な単語を書き入れましょう。音声は 2 回繰り返されます。   ⦿ CD 15

UNIT 7 *Learning to Love Rural Japan*   **39**

Anchor: As rural Japan *continues to**1 struggle with an aging and declining population, local communities are trying to attract visitors from abroad in Akita Prefecture. ❶ One town
(1) (2) (3)
5 (4) (5) (6) to
help foreigners **adapt**. ❷ And as NHK World's Ryo Isojima reports, it's also (1) (2)
(3) (4) (5)
(6).

❶ 語学学校をつくった。

❷ 教室を超えた学びの機会を与えている

10 **Narrator:** A sports day is part of the curriculum at a new Japanese language school in Kosaka. There are 24 students from 10 countries including Indonesia, Mexico and the U.K. The school gives the students one month of unique experiences of the area's culture. Its aim is to **encourage** them to come back someday
15 and **spread the word**, getting more people interested in Akita. The students learn Japanese in the morning. ❸ Then, in the afternoon they (1) (2)
(3) (4) (5)
(6) (7) such as playing with
20 Akita dogs and cooking traditional dishes.

❸ いろいろな活動に参加する

Student: (*While cooking with his friend*) You're good, you're good. You got it.

Matt Williams: Because it was both language and culture. Yeah, I wanted to learn both. I wanted to **interact with locals**, and this
25 is just exactly what I was looking for.

Narrator: Heather Brown is a camera operator living in Los Angeles. She *reached**2 Japan six years ago to shoot a movie. Wanting to learn Japanese, she decided to study at the school.

Heather Brown: I wanted to come to Akita Inaka School because it is beautiful countryside, which is much different from Los Angeles. ❹ It's much more peaceful here, (¹)

(²) (³) (⁴)

(⁵) (⁶).

❹ 本当にここにいるのが楽しいです

Narrator: ❺ Brown is particularly thrilled by the (¹)

(²) (³) (⁴)

(⁵) (⁶) (⁷).

❺ ここの人たちと交流する多くの機会

Michiko Fukui: (*While handing local vegetables to a student*) It's just some beans, but please **help yourself**.

Student: Thank you.

Narrator: Almost everyday, neighbor Michiko Fukui brings locally grown vegetables and some of her home cooking. ❻ At night the students attend parties where they (¹)

(²) (³) (⁴)

(⁵) (⁶).

❻ 会話を通してしぜんに言語を学ぶ

Brown: ❼ Spending time with Fukui-san has been great to (¹) (²) (³)

(⁴) (⁵) (⁶). Um, I'm trying very hard to understand her, and so trying to communicate and speak with her has been very helpful.

❼ 私の日本語の勉強の助けになる

Fukui: Even though she's from another country, she connected with us naturally, as if she'd been living in Kosaka for many years.

Narrator: The climax of the course: Brown and other students wear traditional hanten jackets and join in the local **Bon Festival** dance.

By introducing local culture as well as the Japanese language, the course could even become a **catalyst** to **revitalize** this region. Ryo Isojima, NHK World, Kosaka.

Notes
＊¹ 発音がはっきりしないが、文脈からこの言い方が妥当と判断した
＊² reach の後に at のような発音が聞こえるが、不要

Review the Key Expressions

各問、選択肢から適切な単語を選び、英文を完成させましょう。なお、余分な単語が1語ずつあります。

1. 彼は、全国で知られている有名人がやってきて話をしてくれるというニュースを広めた。

He (＿＿＿＿＿＿) the (＿＿＿＿＿＿) that a national (＿＿＿＿) was
(＿＿＿＿) to (＿＿＿＿) us a (＿＿＿＿).

spread　talk　coming　give　celebrity　word　hold

2. 私が子供のころ、よく両親が外で遊んでもっと運動するように私を促した。

When I was a (＿＿＿＿), my parents (＿＿＿＿) to (＿＿＿＿) me
to (＿＿＿＿) more (＿＿＿＿) by playing (＿＿＿＿).

exercise　kid　outside　earn　used　get　encourage

3. 私たちはうちの技術者を統率できる人〔候補者〕を探しています。

We are (＿＿＿＿＿＿) (＿＿＿＿＿＿) (＿＿＿＿) who (＿＿＿＿)
(＿＿＿＿) our (＿＿＿＿) of engineers.

at　can　looking　lead　candidates　team　for

4. その民間企業は、先細りしている小売店を活性化するために苦労している。

The (＿＿＿＿) (＿＿＿＿) was struggling to (＿＿＿＿＿＿) its
(＿＿＿＿) (＿＿＿＿) business.

retail　prosperous　revitalize　enterprise　dwindling　private

● Discussion Questions

1. Would you join this kind of international language learning program abroad? Why?

2. When you study English, what is most difficult: pronunciation, grammar, vocabulary? Why?

UNIT 8
Advocate for Abduction Issue Remembered

横田滋さんの活動とレガシー

「北朝鮮による拉致被害者家族連絡会」の前代表、横田滋さんが亡くなった。長女めぐみさん（当時13歳）が下校途中に北朝鮮に拉致されたことが判明し、97年に家族会が発足すると代表の座に就いた。長年夫妻で運動の象徴的存在となり、拉致被害者の早期帰還を訴え続けた。近年は体調を崩して入院療養中だった。

NHK WORLD JAPAN
NHK NEWSLINE

YOKOTA SHIGERU: A FATHER'S LASTING LOVE AND LEGACY

● Words & Phrases

○ CD 16

- □ **advocate** 主唱者、先駆的提唱者
- □ **abduction** 拉致、誘拐
- □ **heartache** 苦悩、苦痛
- □ to **snap** 《略式》（スナップ）写真を撮る
- □ **agent** 工作員、諜報員、スパイ
- □ to **uncover** ～をあばく

  The financial scandal case was *uncovered* by a weekly magazine.

  その経済的スキャンダルが週刊誌によってあばかれた。
- □ **skepticism** 懐疑
- □ **breakthrough** 進展
- □ **bilateral** 2国間の、双方の

  The two countries signed a *bilateral* agreement to prevent the smuggling of illegal drugs.

  その両国は、不法薬物の密売を防ぐため2国間協定を結んだ。
- □ **ailing** 病弱な
- □ to **scale back** 率に応じて減らす
- □ **unaccounted for** 行方不明の

以下は、社会問題などに関する用語です。下の枠内から適切な単語を選び、空所に入れましょう。

1. low (   ) rate   少子化
2. (   ) society   高齢化社会
3. (   )   人口減少
4. information (   )   情報格差
5. education-(   ) society   学歴社会
6. (   ) bias   (社会的) 性差別
7. (   ) rights issue   人権問題
8. (   )   贈賄［収賄］
9. power (   )   パワハラ
10. workplace (   )   職場におけるいじめ
11. political (   )   政治腐敗
12. (   ) immigrant   不法入国者
13. (   ) action   集団訴訟
14. (   )   原告、申立人
15. (   )   被告、被告人

aging	birth	bribery	bullying	class
conscious	corruption	defendant	depopulation	gap
gender	harassment	human	illegal	plaintiff

ニュースを見て、内容と合っているものは T、違っているものは F を選びましょう。

1. Yokota Shigeru died 43 years after Megumi was abducted.   [T / F]
2. Megumi's parents learned that she was abducted right after she disappeared.   [T / F]
3. Yokota Shigeru gave talks hundreds of times in various places across Japan.   [T / F]

1 ニュースをもう一度見て、各問の空所に入る適切な選択肢を a 〜 c から選びましょう。

1. Megumi is shown typically ____.
   a. standing with her younger brothers
   b. wearing a kimono in the winter
   c. posing in her school uniform

2. According to North Korea Megumi had ____.
   a. already died
   b. disappeared recently
   c. never been abducted

3. Abductees' families say that they will ____ to solve this issue.
   a. keep pushing the Japanese government
   b. go to North Korea themselves
   c. need the help of the South Korean government

2 右の文字列を並べ替えて単語を作り、各文の空所に入れて意味がとおるようにしましょう。語頭の文字（群）が与えてあるものもあります。

1. Yokota Shigeru was a (**l**   ) figure in the effort to rescue Japanese abductees. [geaind]

2. Megumi disappeared when she was a (   ) high school student. [noiruj]

3. At least 17 Japanese were victims of (**tion**) by North Korea in the 1970s and '80s. [cabud]

4. Yokota Shigeru sent Megumi a (**m**   ) using a short-wave radio in South Korea. [gesaes]

3 CD の音声を聞いて、次ページ News Story の❶〜❼の文中にある空所に適切な単語を書き入れましょう。音声は 2 回繰り返されます。　　　◎ CD 17

Anchor: ❶ A leading figure in the movement to rescue Japanese abductees from North Korea (¹)
(²) (³) (⁴)
(⁵) (⁶). Yokota Shigeru died on
5 Friday, 43 years after his daughter disappeared. ❷ As you'll hear in this next report, he spent half his life (¹)
(²) (³) (⁴)
(⁵).

Narrator: This is how Megumi will be remembered. The image of the
10 teen in her junior high school uniform is well-known across Japan, a symbol of the loss and **heartache** attached to the abduction issue.

About six months after Yokota Shigeru **snapped** the photo, his daughter was gone. It took some 20 years to learn she was
15 abducted by North Korean **agents**. Every detail Yokota **uncovered**, he fought for.

❸ (¹) (²) (³)
(⁴) (⁵) (⁶)
(⁷), there was **skepticism**. The father put a
20 face on a nameless issue. ❹ He traveled the country and gave hundreds of speeches (¹) (²)
(³) (⁴) (⁵)
(⁶) (⁷). Then came a
breakthrough moment.

25 The Japanese government now says North Korean agents abducted at least 17 Japanese citizens in the 1970s and '80s.

❺ At a **bilateral** summit in 2002, North Korea admitted to carrying out abductions, later returning (¹)
(²) (³) (⁴)
30 (⁵) (⁶) (⁷).

❶ 彼の情熱のゆえに記憶されている

❷ 彼女を帰還させようと

❸ 横田さんが最初に (このことで) 声を上げ始めたときは

❹ 彼の娘を救済する手助けをお願いしながら

❺ 拉致した人のうち 5 人

46

Megumi was not among them. North Korea said she had died, but Yokota never lost hope.

In 2006 he went to South Korea and sent her a message over short-wave radio.

⁵ **Yokota Shigeru (Megumi's father):** Megumi, this is your father. My hair has turned white over these years, but please do not worry because your parents are both doing well. People across Japan are waiting for you to come home, as soon as possible. And I believe that day will come in the not-so-distant future. I am ¹⁰ looking forward to when our family can live together. Until then, stay healthy, and take care.

Narrator: ❻ (¹) (²) (³) (⁴) (⁵) (⁶), Yokota would face a new challenge, his **ailing** health. He had to ¹⁵ **scale back** his work but never gave up.

Yokota Shigeru: I want to see Megumi soon.

Narrator: ❼ Yokota died (¹) (²) (³) (⁴) (⁵) (⁶). At least a dozen other abductees remain ²⁰ **unaccounted for**, and each family says they will fight to see the Japanese government do more to bring their loved ones home.

❻ 人生の終わり
  に近づいて

❼ 彼の娘に再び
  会うこともな
  く

Review the Key Expressions

各問、選択肢から適切な単語を選び、英文を完成させましょう。なお、余分な単語が１語ずつあります。

1. 核廃棄物の処理は、これから何年もかけて大きな注意を払って行わなければならない。

The ( ) of ( ) waste must be (_____)

(_____) with ( ) care over many years to ( ).

come   disposal   great   carried   away   nuclear   out

2. そう遠くない将来に、この地域で大きな地震が起こるかもしれないという専門家もいる。

Some ( ) ( ) that a big ( ) may

( ) in this ( ) in the (_____) future.

occur   specialists   earthquake   create   not-so-distant   area   say

3. 執行部にはあなたのような人が必要です。それについてもっとお話ができるのを楽しみにしています。

We ( ) a man like you on our ( ) committee. I'm

(_____) ( ) to ( ) to you ( ) about

it.

more   forward   need   looking   talking   executive   discuss

4. フロリダ州の海岸近くの都市で、分譲マンションが崩壊して間もなく約160人の住民が行方不明になった。

About 160 ( ) were (_____) (_____) shortly after a

( ) building in Florida ( ) in a ( ) near the

coast.

collapsed   city   unaccounted   residents   for   condominium   exploded

● Discussion Questions

1. What recent news event has impacted you a lot? How has it affected you?

2. What country would you most like to live in? Why?

UNIT 9

Clay Artist in Touch with Tradition

パリへ届ける癒しの粘土芸術

クレイアーティスト井上恵子さんの活躍ぶりが、国内外のメディアで大きく取り上げられている。一つひとつが手作りで、色彩豊かな彼女の樹脂粘土工芸作品は別格の芸術品である。人気作品の「お香立て」は繊細に花柄をあしらったもので制作過程も見ていて楽しい。彼女の工房からのリポートである。

CLAY ARTIST IN TOUCH WITH TRADITION

● Words & Phrases

CD 18

□ **recognition** 認めること、承認

She won nation-wide *recognition* as a pianist.

彼女はピアニストとして全国的に認められた。

□ **quintessential** 典型的な

□ **incense stand** お香立て

□ to **captivate** 〜を魅惑［魅了］する

□ to **fascinate** 〜を魅惑［魅了］する

The audience was *fascinated* by the magician's performance.

観衆はマジシャンの演技に魅了された。

□ to **figure** 現れる、目立つ

□ **length** 特定の長さのもの

□ **floral** 花模様の

□ **intricate** 複雑な、込み入った

□ **venue** 開催地、会場

□ **flat**-out 《口語》率直に、完全に

□ **the depth of field** 被写界深度

□ to **accentuate** 〜を強調する

□ **dazzling** 目が眩むほどの

49

Before You Watch

以下は、花の名前を表す語彙です。空所に適切な文字を入れ、下のクロスワードを完成させましょう。

ACROSS

1. ヒマワリ （ s _ _ _ _ _ _ _ _ ）　**2.** ユリ （ _ _ _ _ ）
3. パンジー （ _ _ _ _ _ ）　**4.** アサガオ （ m _ _ _ _ _ _) glory

DOWN

5. コスモス （ _ _ s _ _ _ ）　**6.** カーネーション （ _ _ _ _ _ _ _ _ _ ）
7. スミレ （ _ _ _ _ _ _ ）　**8.** チューリップ （ _ _ _ _ _ ）
9. バラ （ _ _ _ _ ）　**10.** タンポポ （ d _ _ _ _ _ _ _ _ ）
11. アヤメ （ i _ _ _ ）　**12.** サクラ （ _ _ _ _ _ _) blossom

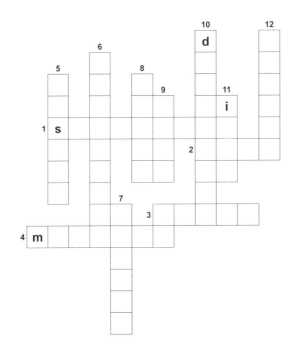

Watch the News   First Viewing

ニュースを見て、内容と合っているものは T、違っているものは F を選びましょう。

1. Inoue had wanted to be a professional artist from the time she was a child.　　[T / F]

2. Inoue's incense stands are made completely of clay.　　[T / F]

3. In the fall, Inoue's works will be displayed in London.　　[T / F]

1 ニュースをもう一度見て、各問の空所に入る適切な選択肢を a 〜 c から選びましょう。

1. Inoue was fascinated by clay art ____.

   a. from the age of 60

   b. when she saw it on TV

   c. after she visited Paris

2. When an offer for an exhibition came from Paris, Inoue ____.

   a. accepted it immediately

   b. completely turned it down

   c. asked for time to make a decision

3. Inoue's work, *Cherry Blossoms*, shows ____.

   a. a fascinating view of layered flower petals

   b. the square pink petals and green leaves

   c. cherry blossoms together with other flowers

2 以下の各情報は井上さんのお香立て制作の行程を示しています。映像の英語をもう一度聞いて、順序よく並べましょう。

1. Stick the slices of clay together in patterns.

2. Combine clay of different colors.

3. Cut the clay into slices.

4. Stretch the clay into long strips.

3 CD の音声を聞いて、次ページ News Story の❶〜❼の文中にある空所に適切な単語を書き入れましょう。音声は 2 回繰り返されます。　　　　　　　　　　◎ CD 19

Anchor: Next, we bring you a report on a Japanese woman who's turned her hobby into serious art and international **recognition**. She's a clay artist, crafting new and original works with a **quintessential** Japanese feel.

5 *Narrator:* These **incense stands** are crafted entirely from clay. Even the colorful patterns are created in the molding process. It's the work of 60-year-old Inoue Keiko, who lives in Miyazaki Prefecture. She has been **captivated** by clay art since she first saw it on television 20 years ago.

10 *Inoue Keiko (Clay artist):* I was **fascinated**, and I wanted to learn the craft. ❶ (¹) (²) (³) (⁴) (⁵) (⁶) (⁷) to me because they're all unique.

❶ どの昨品もかけがえのないものです

15 *Narrator:* Flower motifs, representing the seasons, **figure** highly in Inoue's works. ❷ (¹) (²) (³) (⁴) (⁵) (⁶).

❷ 彼女はまた伝統的な着物の柄を取り入れています

She starts by combining clays of various colors, then stretching 20 them into **lengths**. Next, she cuts them into thin slices, revealing a pattern in cross section. She then sticks the slices together, according to the piece she has in mind, and finishes it by smoothing the surface.

Inoue uses this technique to create **floral** patterns: simple roses 25 and cherry blossoms, or **intricate** ones with complicated lines. This autumn, three of her works will be exhibited at an international art fair in Paris.

The event is one of France's largest art expos, held at the same **venue** that hosts Paris Fashion Week. ❸ At first, Inoue 30 (¹) (²) (³)

❸ 自分の作品を飾ることに関心がなかった

(⁴) (⁵) (⁶)

overseas. She just wanted to keep on making things.

Inoue: ❹ I declined the offer **flat-out** because I didn't realize the

(¹) (²) (³)

5　(⁴) (⁵) (⁶).

❺ When my husband came home that night and I mentioned it,

he scolded me (¹) (²)

(³) (⁴) (⁵)

(⁶). In the end, I decided that I would exhibit

10　my work.

Narrator: This is *Cherry Blossoms*, one of the works Inoue will

exhibit at the expo. Changing color tones **accentuate the depth**

of field, creating the **dazzling** effect of flower petals layered on

top of one another. ❻ It is a (¹)

15　(²) (³) (⁴)

(⁵), and one the artist hopes will captivate

viewers from around the world.

Inoue: ❼ I want (¹) (²)

(³) (⁴) (⁵)

20　(⁶) to people who are suffering from the

pandemic and natural disasters. I hope to exhibit my works in

Paris as soon as possible.

Narrator: Original creations crafted for a new audience. But Inoue is

staying firmly in touch with Japan's artistic traditions.

❹ 催しがそんな
にすばらしい
ことだとは

❺ そんな大きな
機会をのがす
ことについて

❻ 日本の景色の
古典的なスナ
ップショット

❼ 私の作品が癒
しを与えるこ
とを（望みま
す）

Review the Key Expressions

各問、選択肢から適切な単語を選び、英文を完成させましょう。なお、余分な単語が1語ずつあります。

1. 最終的には両者が妥協して、いくつかの要求をあきらめることで話がまとまった。

In (　　　　　　) (　　　　　　), both parties (　　　　　) and agreed to

(　　　　) (　　　　　　) some of their (　　　　　).

<blockquote>give　demands　the　compromised　up　end　get</blockquote>

2. 彼は何年間も糖尿病を患っていたが、食事制限と運動を続けたらずっと気分がよくなった。

He had been (　　　　　　) (　　　　　　) diabetes for (　　　　), but

after (　　　　) and exercise, he (　　　　) (　　　　) better.

<blockquote>much　from　years　felt　after　suffering　dieting</blockquote>

3. ネット上の買い物でこれ以上のセキュリティーの問題を避けるには、できるだけ早くパスワードを変えたほうがいい。

To (　　　　) (　　　　　) security problems while shopping

(　　　　), you (　　　　) change your password (　　　　　)

(　　　　　) as (　　　　).

<blockquote>as　avoid　online　stay　possible　further　soon　should</blockquote>

4. 圭太と直樹は大学で同じクラブに入っていた。卒業後もお互いに連絡を取っていた。

Keita and Naoki (　　　　) (　　　　) the (　　　　) club at

college. (　　　　) after graduation, they (　　　　) in (　　　　)

(　　　　) each other.

<blockquote>to　stayed　belonged　touch　meet　with　same　even</blockquote>

● Discussion Questions

1. What kinds of art are you interested in, fine arts (paintings/photos/sculpture) or performing arts (music/dancing/theater)? Explain.

2. What is your favorite flower? Why? Colors, fragrances, shapes?

UNIT 10
Space Development Board Game

宇宙開発ボードゲーム

鳥取大学が宇宙開発に関した独自のボードゲーム教材を創作した。プレイヤーは宇宙開発に取り組む研究者になりきり、予算を獲得し技術開発を進め、宇宙ミッションの実現をめざす。不況などの経済的条件や政権交代などの政治的条件の下で、技術開発について考えるゲームとして注目されている。

SPACE DEVELOPMENT BOARD GAME

● Words & Phrases

CD 20

☐ **expertise** 専門知識

☐ **constraint** 制約、拘束

☐ to **catch on** 人気を得る、ヒットする

The pop song *caught on* fast among young people.
そのポップスの曲は若い人たちにすぐに人気が出た。

☐ **culmination** 最高点、絶頂、集大成

☐ to **specify** 〜を指定する、明記する

☐ to **throw out** 〜を捨てる

☐ to **stipulate** 〜を要求する

☐ **lucrative** 利益の上がる

Tom inherited a *lucrative* business from his father.
トムは父親から利益の上がる事業を引き継いだ。

☐ **solely** 単に

☐ to **allocate** （金額・役割など）を割り当てる

☐ **instructive** ためになる、教育的な

以下は、天体や宇宙（開発）などに関する語彙です。下の枠内から適切な単語を選び、空所に入れましょう。なお余分な選択肢もあります。

1. 銀河　(　　　　　　　)
2. 太陽系　(　　　　　　　) system
3. 惑星　(　　　　　　)
4. 水星　(　　　　　)
5. 金星　(　　　　　)
6. 火星　(　　　　　)
7. 木星　(　　　　　)
8. 土星　(　　　　　)
9. 地球の自転 the (　　　　　) of the earth
10. 大気圏　earth's (　　　　　)
11. 大気圏外　(　　　　　　) space
12. 宇宙飛行　space (　　　　　)
13. 宇宙飛行士　(　　　　　)
14. 宇宙探査　space (　　　　　)
15. 宇宙服　(　　　　)
16. 人工衛星　artificial (　　　　)
17. 軌道　(　　　　)
18. 打ち上げ　(　　　　)
19. 着地　(　　　　)
20. 軟着陸　(　　　　) landing

astronaut	atmosphere	comet	exploration
flight	galaxy	Jupiter	launch	Mars
Mercury	Neptune	orbit	outer	planet
rotation	satellite	Saturn	soft	solar
spacesuit	touchdown	Uranus	Venus	

ニュースを見て、内容と合っているものは T、違っているものは F を選びましょう。

1. Two researchers designed and produced this board game. [T / F]
2. This game is particularly popular among young businesspeople. [T / F]
3. The player wins the game if he/she can launch the most rockets within budget. [T / F]

Understand the News

Second Viewing

1 ニュースをもう一度見て、各問の空所に入る適切な選択肢を a 〜 c から選びましょう。

1. To successfully launch rockets ____.
   a. a project manager is necessary
   b. technicians take care of most procedures
   c. government leadership must remain the same

2. This new board game has rules quite close to those of ____.
   a. chess
   b. poker
   c. bingo

3. Engineers tend to think only about the ____.
   a. weather on the day of the launch
   b. government's budget for salaries
   c. technological aspects of their projects

2 右の文字列を並べ替えて単語を作り、各文の空所に入れて意味がとおるようにしましょう。語頭の文字が与えてあるものもあります。

1. A (**b**   ) is the amount of money available to a person/an organization for a certain project during a set period of time.   [tegud]

2. This new board game is (   ) on with students. 《進行形》   [ctahcing]

3. All the (**p**   ) in this board game try to launch rockets. 《複数形》[erayls]

4. A change of (   ) means a change in governments.   [eorwp]

3 CD の音声を聞いて、次ページ News Story の ❶〜❼の文中にある空所に適切な単語を書き入れましょう。音声は 2 回繰り返されます。   ◎ CD 21

Anchor: Launching a rocket requires not just technological **expertise** but also careful thinking about budget **constraints**. Now two researchers have created a board game that encourages people to reflect on the impact of real world events on project finances.

5　　　And it's **catching on** with students and engineers.

Narrator: (*A video of a rocket lifting off*) It's the **culmination** of years of hard work and planning. Every rocket launch requires a project manager who can keep the work within budget. Two university researchers have created a board game to increase

10　　　awareness about the challenges involved.

Haruhiko Maenami *(Former Assoc. Prof., Tottori University):* ❶ I hope it makes people think about the relationship (¹) (²) (³) (⁴) (⁵).

❶ 科学技術と社会の間の〜

15 **Narrator:** ❷ Players pick a card (¹) (²) (³) (⁴) (⁵). Then, they get a series of cards that **specify** their costs across six categories, such as the engine and battery. Players have to **throw out** the cards that **stipulate** costs beyond their budget.

❷ 彼らの予算を伝える

20　　　The rules are similar to those of poker. A rocket launch becomes possible when players attain a certain combination of colors and numbers. They also get cards alerting them to political, economic or social developments, such as change of government or global depression. These put further limitations

25　　　on their budgets. The player who successfully launches the most rockets within budget is the winner.

This major electronics maker is aiming to enter the **lucrative** space industry. ❸ Some of (¹) (²) (³) (⁴)

30　　　(⁵) (⁶).

❸ 社員がそのゲームを試してみた

❹ The engineers are used to focusing **solely** on the technological side of projects, but the game (¹)
(²) (³) (⁴)
(⁵).

Gameplayer 1: (*Reading a card*) A change of power. ❺ Support for the project was increasing, but the change in government (¹) (²) (³)
(⁴) (⁵).

Gameplayer 2: (*Reading a card*) A supplementary *initial**¹ budget has been **allocated**. More money.

Narrator: The engineers learned that the changes in the wider world can have an impact on the technical work they do in their offices.

Man: My research and development is really meaningful, but I can also see how important it is to promote what we're doing to the people who decide our budgets.

Woman: ❻ I learned that we need to (¹)
(²) (³) (⁴)
(⁵) (⁶).

Narrator: ❼ People who've tried the game say (¹)
(²) (³) (⁴)
(⁵) (⁶). That's a good sign for the developers who are considering *to sell**² it to the public.

❹ 彼らに新たな視点を身につけさせた

❺ 今度は、予算の削減を意味する

❻ 社会で起こっていることをもっと意識する

❼ ためになるばかりではなく、楽しい

Notes

*¹ *initial* は不要だと思われる

*² *to sell* ではなく selling が文法的なかたち

Review the Key Expressions

各問、選択肢から適切な単語を選び、英文を完成させましょう。なお、余分な単語が1語ずつあります。

1. この科目は単に仕事上だけではなく、私生活でも人々の役に立つ。

This course will (　　　　　　) people (＿＿＿＿＿＿＿) (＿＿＿＿＿＿＿) in their

careers, (＿＿＿＿＿＿) also in their (　　　　　　) (　　　　　　).

> not　help　lives　just　but　quite　personal

2. そのベンチャー企業は、新形式の室内運動用 VR ゴーグルを発明して、それらはすぐに人気が出た。

The venture firm (　　　　　　) a new (　　　　　　) of VR (　　　　　　) for

(　　　　　　) exercise and they immediately (＿＿＿＿＿＿＿) (＿＿＿＿＿＿＿).

> caught　became　goggles　indoor　on　invented　style

3. 古いおもちゃは捨てずに、ネット販売してみたらどうですか。

(　　　　　　) than (＿＿＿＿＿＿) (＿＿＿＿＿＿) your old toys,

(　　　　　　) (　　　　　　) you sell them (　　　　　　)?

> out　don't　throwing　online　why　rather　use

4. 医師に注意されるまで、ジョージは電子たばこの危険性に気付いていなかった。

Before George (　　　　　　) (　　　　　　) by his doctor, he (　　　　　　)

not (＿＿＿＿＿＿) (＿＿＿＿＿＿) of the (　　　　　　) of smoking e-cigarettes.

> had　warned　realize　aware　risks　been　was

● Discussion Questions

1. Do you like games? If yes, what game do you like best? Explain why. If not, why not?

2. Would you like to be an astronaut or a scientist? Why?

Tatami Takes on New Shapes and Sizes

デザイン畳

近年は住宅の西洋化のあおりを受け、畳業界が需要を減らしている。そんな中、岐阜県の畳店では、現代の内装に合わせた畳を開発し始めた。鋭角処理や曲線のある畳はずいぶん手間がかかるが、でき栄えは斬新で芸術性に富み注目を集めている。伝統を守りながら新しい技術を融合させる創作の日々をリポートする。

TATAMI TAKES ON NEW SHAPES AND SIZES

● Words & Phrases

CD 22

- [ ] to **take on**　〜を取り入れる
- [ ] **staple**　欠かせないもの、中心的なもの
- [ ] to **come in**　手に入る

  This deodorant *comes in* three varieties: stick, roll-on and spray.

  このデオドラントはスティック、ロールオン、スプレー式の3種類がある。
- [ ] **rectangular**　長方形の
- [ ] **figure**　形態
- [ ] to **weave**　〜を織り込む
- [ ] to **work on**　〜に取り組む、従事する

  The students are *working on* their presentation for an international conference.

  学生たちは国際的な会議のプレゼンに取り組んでいる。
- [ ] to **take over**　〜の後を継ぐ
- [ ] **eye**-**opener**　《口語》驚くべき発見
- [ ] **spice**　趣、おもしろみ
- [ ] **hexagonal**　六角形の
- [ ] **celebrity**　有名人

以下は、語源に関する問題です。下の選択肢から日本語を選び表の空所に入れましょう。

	語彙	意味	形態素	意味	形態素	意味	形態素	意味
例	hexagon	六角形	hexa-	6	-gon	角度		
1	rectangle	( )	rect-	( )	-angle	角度		
2	sociology	( )	soci-	社会	-ology	( )		
3	president	社長、会長	pre-	( )	-sid-	( )	-ent	( )
4	percent	パーセント	per-	( )	-cent	( )		
5	tripod	( )	tri-	3	-pod	( )		
6	suspend	( )	sus-	( )	-pend	( )		
7	portable	ポータブル	port-	( )	-able	〜できる		
8	manicure	マニキュア	mani-	( )	-cure	( )		
9	supervisor	管理者	super-	( )	-vis-	( )	-or	人
10	library	図書館	libr-	( )	-ary	〜に関する場所		
11	describe	記述する	de-	下へ	-scribe	( )		
12	postpone	( )	post-	( )	-pone	( )		

脚・足	後ろに	延期する	置く	書く	〜学	三脚
社会学	下に	すわる	世話	中断する	長方形	つるす
手	〜につき	〜の上を	運ぶ	人	100	本
前に	まっすぐな	見る				

ニュースを見て、内容と合っているものは T、違っているものは F を選びましょう。

1. Kenji Yamada is the first and current owner of this tatami shop.   [T / F]

2. Yamada says that not many homes have traditional Japanese-style rooms.   [T / F]

3. The owner of the old inn wanted to buy cooking spices from Yamada.   [T / F]

1 ニュースをもう一度見て、各問の空所に入る適切な選択肢を a〜c から選びましょう。

1. Yamada's new-style tatami costs ____.

   a. as much as the traditional kind

   b. half the price of original-style tatami

   c. more than double that of ordinary tatami

2. Yamada is starting to work on designing ____.

   a. pictures of famous people using specially-shaped tatami

   b. zoo animals on multi-colored tatami mats

   c. tatami seats for sports car interiors

3. Yamada is trying to ____.

   a. change to a different profession

   b. find a business partner who lives in the U.S.A.

   c. develop an overseas tatami market

2 右の文字列を並べ替えて単語を作り、各文の空所に入れて意味がとおるようにしましょう。語頭の文字（群）が与えてあるものもあります。

1. Traditional tatami is (**r**   ) in shape.   [largutanec]

2. Ohashi asked Yamada to install special tatami mats in her (   ) room.

                                                       [viglin]

3. The traditional local inn is (   ) years old.   [tenyni]

4. The word "(**ce**   )"《複数形》 means famous people.   [esritileb]

3 CD の音声を聞いて、次ページ News Story の❶〜❼の文中にある空所に適切な単語を書き入れましょう。音声は 2 回繰り返されます。　　　　　　　◎ CD 23

Anchor: Tatami flooring has long been a **staple** in traditional Japanese homes. ❶ They usually **come in rectangular** shapes and

(　　　　¹) (　　　　²) (　　　　³)

(　　　　⁴) (　　　　⁵) (　　　　⁶) to any

5　space. But one maker is exploring new **figures** and giving tatami a modern twist. NHK World's Ayako Sasa has the story.

Narrator: For Kenji Yamada, tatami is **woven** deep into his family's history. He is the fifth generation owner of a shop in Gifu Prefecture. The mats he's currently **working on** come together

10　to form a dragon.

Yamada started off working in housing construction. He saw firsthand how most homes these days have no Japanese-style rooms. ❷ He realized if tatami makers didn't adapt, they

(　　　　¹) (　　　　²) (　　　　³)

15　(　　　　⁴) (　　　　⁵) (　　　　⁶) . He

eventually **took over** the family business. One day a customer asked him to fit the back of a car with tatami. He says the experience was a real **eye-opener**.

Kenji Yamada (Tatami craftsman): ❸ The fit (　　　　¹)

20　(　　　　²) (　　　　³) (　　　　⁴)

(　　　　⁵) (　　　　⁶). It made me think, "You know, maybe I can do more with my tatami."

Narrator: ❹ He started to experiment, and (　　　　¹)

(　　　　²) (　　　　³) (　　　　⁴)

25　(　　　　⁵) (　　　　⁶) (　　　　⁷).

❺ The prices are more than twice *that** of normal tatami, but

(　　　　¹) (　　　　²) (　　　　³)

(　　　　⁴) (　　　　⁵) (　　　　⁶)

around the country.

30　Miho Ohashi asked Yamada to install tatami in her apartment.

❶ 少し心地よさ
を加えること
ができる

❷ やがて廃業し
てしまうかも
しれない

❸ 予想よりはる
かにうまくい
った

❹ 彼のユニーク
なデザインは
すぐにうまく
いった

❺ 彼はまだ、お
客さんから注
文を受けてい
る

She wanted the mats to add something different to her living room.

Miho Ohashi: I chose this tatami because I wanted something that looked different, depending on lighting. It's come out better than I could have hoped.

Narrator: The owner of this inn wanted to add some modern **spice** to the 90-year-old building. He turned to Yamada. Over 400 tatami mats later, the property has a completely different atmosphere.

Now Yamada is moving onto the next big thing. He is working on designs that use small, **hexagonal** mats to form **celebrity** faces.

Yamada: ❻ We are only just scratching the surface of (^{1}) (^{2}) (^{3}) (^{4}) (^{5}) (^{6}). We want to take it further and do even more.

Narrator: ❼ Yamada (^{1}) (^{2}) (^{3}) (^{4}) (^{5}) (^{6}), setting his sights firmly on overseas customers. For him, it seems like the natural next step in the evolution of tatami. Ayako Sasa, NHK World, Gifu.

❻ 私たちが畳を使ってやれること

❼ 英語のウェブサイトを作った

Note

＊複数形を受けるので、文法的には those にする

Review the Key Expressions

各問、選択肢から適切な単語を選び、英文を完成させましょう。なお、余分な単語が1語ずつあります。

1. 1日に30分歩くだけで、寿命を何年も延ばせる［寿命に何年も<u>加える</u>］可能性がある。

(　　　　　　　) walking (　　　　　　) an (　　　　　　) a day can

(＿＿＿＿＿＿＿) (　　　　　　　) to your (　　　　　　).

> quarter　life　even　hour　years　add　half

2. 私たちは、観光客が行ってみたいと思うような町起こし<u>に取り組む</u>ことが必要だ。

It is (　　　　　) for (　　　　　) to (＿＿＿＿＿＿) on (　　　　　　　)

our town (　　　　　) that (　　　　　) will want to visit.

> tourists　us　necessary　work　so　installing　revitalizing

3. 社長の孫息子が<u>後を継いで</u>から、その企業の再編に懸命に取り組んだ。

(　　　　　) the president's grandson (＿＿＿＿＿＿) (＿＿＿＿＿＿), he

(　　　　　) hard on (　　　　　) the (　　　　　).

> took　business　after　worked　restructuring　looked　over

4. 発展途上国を訪れると本当に<u>驚きの発見</u>がありうる。みんな、水道水や進んだ医療が身近にあるわけではないのだ。

(　　　　　) developing countries (　　　　　) be a real (＿＿＿＿＿＿).

(　　　　　) everyone has (　　　　　) to (　　　　　) water or modern

(　　　　　) services.

> running　visiting　access　not　medical　can　all　eye-opener

● Discussion Questions

1. What do you think of the artistic tatami in different shapes? Would you buy them from Yamada? Why?

2. What Japanese traditions would you like to pass down to your grandchildren? Why?

A Runway to a New Start

義足のランウェイ

Amputee Venus（切断ヴィーナス）の活動が注目されている。事故や病気などが原因で、脚を切断された女性たちが、障がいを隠さず個性的な義足をつけ、それを楽しむものとして提唱している。この意識改革は障がい者だけの問題ではなく、健常者も先入観を取り払うことで、お互いにひとりの人間として尊重できるようになるのが本来の社会である。
（写真：海音〈あまね〉さん。東京五輪の閉会式にも登場した、若手の義足モデル。）

A RUNWAY TO A NEW START

● Words & Phrases

◎ CD 24

- ☐ **runway**　ステージ
- ☐ to **be supposed to**　〜する予定である
- ☐ to **take place**　開催される
- ☐ **catwalk**　（ファッションショーの）細長いステージ
- ☐ **one's outlook on life**　人生観
- ☐ to **strut**　気取って歩く
- ☐ **prosthesis**　義足、義肢、補装具
- ☐ to **stream**　〜をストリーム配信する
- ☐ to **contract**　（重い病気）にかかる

　　He *contracted* tuberculosis and was hospitalized.
　　彼は結核にかかって入院した。

- ☐ to **amputate**　（手、脚など）を切断する

　　He had a traffic accident and had to have his left leg *amputated*.
　　彼は交通事故に遭い、左脚を切断しなければいけなかった。

- ☐ **prosthetist**　義肢装具士

Before You Watch

以下は、衣服に関する語彙です。日本語に合う英語の語彙を空所に書きましょう（複数形が可能なものはそれを入れる）。語頭の文字が与えてあるものもあります。

1. 女性用衣類（集合的に）　　women's (**c**　　　　　　)
2. 学校の制服　　　　　　　school (**u**　　　　　　)
3. ワンピース　　　　　　　(**d**　　　　　　)
4. 作業服　　　　　　　　　(**w**　　　　　　) clothes
5. 男性用スーツ（一着）　　men's (　　　　　　　　)
6. 上着　　　　　　　　　　(**j**　　　　　　)
7. ベスト　　　　　　　　　(　　　　　　　)
8. 上半身に着る衣服　　　　(**t**　　　　　　)
9. 下半身にはく衣服　　　　(**b**　　　　　　)
10. ブラウス　　　　　　　　(　　　　　　　)
11. スウェット　　　　　　　(　　　　　　　)
12. ジーンズ　　　　　　　　(　　　　　　　)
13. ズボン　　　　　　　　　(**p**　　　　　　)
14. Tシャツ　　　　　　　　(　　　　　　　)
15. パジャマ　　　　　　　　(　　　　　　　)
16. 下着　　　　　　　　　　(**u**　　　　　　)

Watch the News   First Viewing

ニュースを見て、内容と合っているものは T、違っているものは F を選びましょう。

1. Because of the pandemic, the Amputee Venus Show took place online.　　　[T / F]

2. In high school, Amane had her uniform skirt made longer.　　　[T / F]

3. Amane was the last model to appear in the Amputee Venus Show.　　　[T / F]

1 ニュースをもう一度見て、各問の空所に入る適切な選択肢を a 〜 c から選びましょう。

1. Ochi Takao ____.

   a. is a prosthetist who made artificial legs for the participants

   b. is a photographer and organizer of the Amputee Venus Show

   c. was the principal when Amane attended his high school

2. Amane had to have her right leg amputated ____.

   a. when she turned 18 years old

   b. due to a traffic accident six years ago

   c. because she contracted an illness

3. Amane decided to show her prosthesis in public ____.

   a. after she saw a disabled model at the Paralympics

   b. while she was working as a child model

   c. when she learned about a beautiful silver prosthesis

2 右の文字列を並べ替えて単語を作り、各文の空所に入れて意味がとおるようにしましょう。語頭の文字（群）が与えてあるものもあります。

1. A (r   ) is a long, narrow walkway extending from the main stage of a fashion show.   [awyun]

2. A (   ) is someone paid to wear new fashions at shows to promote clothing sales.   [dleom]

3. In the fashion show, Amane was able to display her prosthesis with a (   ) on her face.   [lesim]

4. At the closing (ce   ) of the Paralympics, Amane saw a woman proudly wearing her prosthesis on stage.   [yrenmo]

3 CD の音声を聞いて、次ページ News Story の❶〜❼の文中にある空所に適切な単語を書き入れましょう。音声は 2 回繰り返されます。   ◉ CD 25

Anchor: ❶ Now the pandemic may have postponed the Tokyo Paralympic Games, but it (¹) (²) (³) (⁴) (⁵) (⁶). ❷ On the day the opening ceremony **was supposed to take place**, Paralympians and models (¹) (²) (³) (⁴) (⁵) (⁶). In our next story, we meet a model who took to the **catwalk** as a way to challenge **her outlook on life**.

❶ （〜が）祭典を中止にしなかった

❷ 珍しいファッションショーに参加する

Narrator: *Women**¹ **strut** down a runway, proudly displaying what they all have in common: talent, beauty, strength and *prosthesis**². To prevent the possible spread of coronavirus, the Amputee Venus Show was held without an audience and **streamed** live online. Photographer Ochi Takao planned this event.

Ochi Takao (Photographer): Well, I've seen the dynamic appearance of Paralympians and athletes with prosthetic legs while shooting, so I was shocked to know there are quite a few people hiding their *prosthesis**³.

Narrator: Eighteen-year-old Amane took part in the show. She used to be a child model, but she had to give up her work six years ago after **contracting** an illness that resulted in having her right leg **amputated**. Since then, she has been hiding her prosthesis.

Amane (Model): I didn't like the fact that I wasn't an ordinary person, *with a prosthesis**⁴, so I hid it. My school uniform was supposed to be about this length, but I had it *made**⁵ longer.

Narrator: ❸ Four years ago (¹) (²) (³) (⁴) (⁵) (⁶). During the closing ceremony of the Paralympics, she watched a model with an artificial leg appear

❸ 気持ちが変わった

on the stage.

Amane: It was really cool to see her walking proudly with [a]*6 prosthesis. I thought it would be okay to show a prosthesis.

Narrator: Amane decided to take part in the Amputee Venus Show.
5 She visited [a]*7 **prosthetist** who created a beautiful silver prosthesis for her lower leg.

Usui Fumio (Prosthetist): (*He talks to Amane.*) How about the length? Is this *leg**8 okay? (*He starts walking with Amane.*) ❹ Do you think we can (1) (2)
10 (3) (4) (5) (6)?

❹ これでステージを歩く

Amane: Yes.

Narrator: ❺ (1) (2) (3) (4) (5) (6),
15 Amane was the first on stage. She appeared confident and cool in a short skirt she couldn't wear when she was in high school.

❺ 出演の日に

Amane: ❻ (1) (2) (3) (4) (5). ❼ I (1) (2) (3) (4)
20 (5). I think I was able to walk with a smile as a new self.

❻ 自信をもって歩くことができた

❼ 生まれ変わったように感じた

Narrator: The Amputee Venus Show doesn't focus on what some might see as missing, *and**9 instead opens up a whole new world of opportunities for the participants.

Notes
＊¹ 正しくは、発音が複数形 [wímən] になるべき
＊² 複数形 *prostheses* が期待されるところ
＊³ ここも ＊² と同様
＊⁴ *with a prosthesis* は 6 語前の that の次に置かれるほうがしぜん
＊⁵ made の後に it のような音が聞こえるが不要
＊⁶ a が必要
＊⁷ a が必要
＊⁸ 発音が不明瞭だが leg だと意味をなす
＊⁹ but が期待されるところ

Review the Key Expressions

各問、選択肢から適切な単語を選び、英文を完成させましょう。なお、余分な単語が 1 語ずつあります。

1. 私たちの会社で働きたい 5 人の人たちと、今日オンラインで面接を<u>予定しています</u>。

We ( ) ( ) to have online ( ) today

( ) five people ( ) are ( ) in

( ) for our company.

interested   have   supposed   who   interviews   with   working   are

2. 毎年行われている国際スピーチコンテストが、その大学の講堂で<u>開催される</u>。

The ( ) international ( ) ( ) will

( ) ( ) in the university ( ).

speech   centennial   place   contest   auditorium   take   annual

3. 昔は英語とドイツ語にはもっと<u>共通点があった</u>。例えば英語の名詞は今日のドイツ語のように文法上の性があった。

( ) ago, English and German languages ( ) more

( ) ( ). For example, English nouns had ( )

just ( ) German nouns do today.

in   genders   had   share   common   like   long

4. この辺では、子供がスマホに時間をとられ過ぎて前より社会行事に<u>参加し</u>なくなっていますか。

Do ( ) kids in this community ( ) ( ) in

( ) events because they spend too ( ) ( ) on

their smartphones?

social   time   part   much   associate   take   fewer

● Discussion Questions

1. Name one activity able-bodied and disabled people can enjoy together. Explain.

2. Everyone has some kind of talent. What is one thing that you are pretty good at? Explain.

Teaching about Black Lives Matter

人種差別をなくす

ジョージ・フロイドさんは合衆国ミネアポリス市で逮捕され、警察の過剰な身体的拘束により死亡したアフリカ系アメリカ人である。この事件に反応して黒人への警官の暴力的対応への抗議デモが、世界中に拡大した。日本で英語を教えるウィルソンさんは今回、黒人への人種差別について特別授業を行い命の尊さを訴えた。

● **Words & Phrases**

○ CD 26

- [ ] to **matter** 重要である

    We need to think about what *matters* most for our company to survive.

    私たちは、会社が生き残るために何が最も大事なのか考える必要がある。

- [ ] to **trigger** 〜の引き金を引く

    Stress can *trigger* many physical and psychological problems.

    ストレスは多くの身体的、精神的問題の引き金になったりする。

- [ ] **injustice** 不正、不公平

- [ ] to **speak out** 遠慮なく話す

- [ ] **discrimination** 差別

- [ ] **racism** 人種差別、人種的偏見

- [ ] **seventh grader** 7年生、中学1年生

- [ ] **prejudice** 偏見

- [ ] to **cross barriers** 障壁を乗り越える

Before You Watch

以下は、社会・文化問題や自然・環境問題に関する表現です。下の枠内から適切な単語を
選び、空所に入れましょう。選択肢はすべて小文字にしてあります。

1. 《プラカード》「差別主義者の暴力を止めよう」 STOP (   ) VIOLENCE

2. すべての人が性別による差別をなくさなければならない。
All people have to end (   ) based on (   ).

3. ほとんどの国は核兵器を諦めようとしない。
Most countries will not give up their (   ) (   ).

4. 地球温暖化は、長い間行われてきた。
(   ) (   ) has been going on for a long time.

5. いろいろな種類の動植物のバランスを崩さないように、絶滅危惧種を救うことが緊急
に必要だ。
Saving (   ) (   ) is an urgent need to avoid upsetting
the balance among various kinds of animals and plants.

6. いじめ問題にはきっぱりと終止符を打ってほしいと切に願う。
I really hope we can put an (   ) to (   ) once and for all.

7. 貧困と武装紛争は、文明の始まりからずっと続いている大きな社会問題だ。
(   ) and armed (   ) have been major social problems
since the beginning of civilization.

bullying	conflicts	discrimination	end
endangered	gender	global	nuclear
poverty	racist	species	warming	weapons

Watch the News　　　　　　　　　　**First Viewing**

ニュースを見て、内容と合っているものはT、違っているものはFを選びましょう。

1. Wilson wondered how she could explain to students about racial problems.   [T / F]

2. Wilson asked her students why there are still racists in the world.   [T / F]

3. Wilson was shocked that her feelings were not understood well in English.   [T / F]

1 ニュースをもう一度見て、各問の空所に入る適切な選択肢を a〜c から選びましょう。

1. Wilson first hesitated to teach a special class because _____.

   a. she was not confident about her Japanese

   b. she didn't want her students to feel upset

   c. talking about racial matters is prohibited in schools

2. The school made a decision to have a special class for _____.

   a. all junior high students

   b. the first year students

   c. the students and their parents

3. Wilson _____.

   a. thought that she had forced her opinions on the Japanese youngsters

   b. wanted to talk about racism with college students

   c. hoped she'd helped students express their feelings

2 以下はニュースの概要です。空所に適切な単語を書き入れましょう。語頭の文字（群）は与えてあります。

Recently, an unarmed African-American died after he was arrested by the police in the U.S. This incident caused global protests against (r _____ ¹) discrimination. Mahogany Wilson is an (E _____ ²) teacher working in a Japanese (j _____ ³) high school. She asked her school if she could talk about this matter in class. The school permitted her to give a special class to (s _____ ⁴) graders. Students realized that (r _____ ⁵) still exists against Black people. Thanks to her talk, students realized that people around the world should work together to fight against all kinds of discrimination.

3 CD の音声を聞いて、次ページ News Story の❶〜❼の文中にある空所に適切な単語を書き入れましょう。音声は 2 回繰り返されます。　　　　　　　⊙ CD 27

Anchor: The death of an unarmed Black man by U.S. police in May **triggered** global protests against racial **injustice**. ❶ And here in Japan (^{1}) (^{2}) (^{3}) (^{4}) (^{5})

5 (^{6}) both large and small. Japanese tennis star Osaka Naomi is using her platform to ***speak out****[1] against racial **discrimination**. ❷ And as NHK World's Honda Mina reports, (^{1}) (^{2}) (^{3}) in western Japan (^{4}) (^{5})

10 (^{6}) (^{7}).

Mahogany Wilson **(Assistant Language Teacher, Kamogawa Junior High School):** I keep thinking, "What can I do to make the difference? What change can I *do*,*[2] being so far away from America?"

15 *Narrator:* Mahogany Wilson is from Missouri and started teaching English in Japan last April. But she considered a timely lesson to offer at school. ❸ She (^{1}) (^{2}) (^{3}) (^{4}) (^{5}) (^{6}) about **racism**.

20 *Wilson:* I don't want to make anyone feel uncomfortable. I care about the way they feel, so even if I don't feel okay, I don't want to make my problem their problem....

Narrator: Wilson asked her colleagues at the middle school to help her design programs that would help students think about
25 racism. In response, the school decided to hold a special class for **seventh graders**.

Wilson: So we are going to talk about Black Lives Matter Too.

Narrator: First, she introduced the story of George Floyd and had the students think about why he was killed.

30 *Wilson:* (*She shows three pictures.*) Raise your hand if you think it

❶ 犠牲者のための社会的運動が行われて[見られて]いる

❷ （〜の）英語教師が同じことをしている

❸ 彼女は遠慮のない意見を言っていいのかどうかと考えた

76

was for c), being Black.... Well, you are all correct.

Narrator: She asked the students why racism still exists.

Student 1: ❹ I think it's (¹) (²)

(³) (⁴) (⁵)

5   (⁶).

Student 2: I think in the United States people have **prejudice** towards

Black people.

Narrator: Finally, Wilson asked the students what they can do, the

question she wanted them to reflect on most.

10 ***Student 3:*** Based on what the teacher said, in the U.S. there's

discrimination against people with black skin, different hair and

so on. ❺ I found it odd (¹) (²)

(³) (⁴) (⁵).

Student 4: We can start getting rid of discrimination even with very

15   small steps, such as greeting other people so you feel kinder

toward each other.

Wilson: ❻ When we stand together, (¹)

(²) (³) (⁴)

(⁵). ❼ (¹) (²)

20   (³) (⁴).

I have many feelings about teaching this class today. I was

completely shocked that they can *make**3* some good

explanation[*s*].*4

Narrator: Mahogany hopes her lessons **crossed barriers** of culture

25   and language to help her students find their own voices. Honda

Mina, NHK World.

❹ まだ人種差別
をする人がい
るから

❺ 差別が多くあ
ること

❻ 自分たちには
変化を起こせ
る

❼ ご清聴ありが
とうございま
す

Notes

*1 speak out の後に母音のような発音が聞こえるが、不要である。

*2 cause か make のほうがよい

*3 give のほうがよりしぜん

*4 -s が必要

Review the Key Expressions

各問、選択肢から適切な単語を選び、英文を完成させましょう。なお、余分な単語が1語ずつあります。

1. その消費者団体は、遺伝子組み換え食品の生産に反対の声を<u>上げている</u>。

The (   ) group is (_____) (_____) against the

(   ) of (   ) (   ) foods.

> genetically   production   consumer   speaking   retailer   modified   out

2. 今私が言ったことが理解出なかったら、<u>手を挙げて</u>ご自由に質問をしてください。

If you don't (   ) (   ) I have just said, (_____) your

(_____) and feel (   ) to ask me (   ) questions.

> raise   understand   stand   any   hand   free   what

3. （あなたの）お父さんは、あなたの帰りが時々遅いと叱りました。あなたのことをとても<u>心配した</u>からです。

Your father (   ) you about (   ) (   ) late so

often, because he (_____) so (   ) (_____) you.

> angry   about   coming   cared   home   scolded   much

4. 祖父と祖母は年を取るにつれて、所持品をどんどん［もっと］<u>捨て</u>ようとしている。

(   ) my grandparents (   ) (   ), they are trying

to <u>get</u> (_____) (_____) more of their (   ).

> get   rid   older   as   out   possessions   of

● Discussion Questions

1. Osaka Naomi wore masks with Black victims' names on them when she appeared on the tennis court. What is your opinion of this?

2. Name a global problem that people have to take action on as soon as possible. Explain why.

Tochigi Gourd Magic

意外なかんぴょう活用
—— 栃木発

ひょうたんが楽器やスピーカーとして利用されたり、かんぴょうが医療で皮膚の縫合練習キットとして開発されたりと従来の用途とは違う使い方が注目を集めている。特に後者は自治医科大が産学連携で国産キットの製品化を目指す。利点は何か、またどのような経緯でこのアイデアが啓発されたのかリポートをする。

TOCHIGI GOURD MAGIC

● Words & Phrases

CD 28

- ☐ **bottle gourd**　ひょうたん
- ☐ to **harness**　（自然の力）を利用する
- ☐ to **enhance**　（価値・性能など）を高める

  The author's new book will *enhance* his reputation.
  この著者の新しい本が彼の評判を高めるだろう。

- ☐ **hollow**　空っぽの、空洞の
- ☐ **fluff**　ふわふわしたかたまり
- ☐ to **suture**　（傷口など）を縫い合わせる
- ☐ to **rehydrate**　（乾燥食品など）を水を加えて元に戻す
- ☐ **strip**　（剝いた皮などの）細長いもの
- ☐ **taut**　ピンと張った
- ☐ **brainchild**　頭脳の産物、創作品
- ☐ **aspiring**　意欲的な、向上心のある

  The aide to the governor is an *aspiring* politician.
  その県知事の側近は意欲的な政治家です。

- ☐ to **penetrate**　突き刺さる
- ☐ **culinary**　料理に関する

以下は、すしネタ（sushi topping）に関する表現です。下の枠内から適切な単語を選び、空所に入れましょう。

1. かんぴょう巻き   dried (   ) roll
2. マグロ (赤身)   (   ) tuna
3. マグロ (トロ)   (   ) tuna
4. ハマチ   young (   )
5. サバ   (   )
6. タイ   sea (   )
7. サケ   (   )
8. ヒラメ   (   )
9. イワシ   (   )
10. ウナギ   (   )
11. ホタテ   (   )
12. アワビ   (   )
13. イカ   (   )
14. タコ   (   )
15. エビ   (   )
16. イクラ   salmon (   )

abalone	bream	eel	fatty	flounder
gourd	lean	mackerel	octopus	roe	salmon
sardine	scallop	shrimp	squid	yellowtail

Watch the News   First Viewing

ニュースを見て、内容と合っているものは T、違っているものは F を選びましょう。

1. Almost all *kanpyo* is produced in Ibaraki Prefecture.   [T / F]

2. Takahashi Akira learned that gourds are used as musical instruments.   [T / F]

3. Dr. Mato realized that *kanpyo*'s texture feels like people's skin.   [T / F]

1 ニュースをもう一度見て、各問の空所に入る適切な選択肢を a 〜 c から選びましょう。

1. *Kanpyo* ____.
   a. is made of a bottle gourd
   b. contains dried watermelon skin
   c. resembles tropical fruit

2. The clear sound produced in dried bottle gourds is due to the ____.
   a. size and shape of the fruit
   b. temperature in the place they were grown
   c. cotton-like material which is inside

3. Dr. Mato guessed that *kanpyo* might be used in medicine when he was ____.
   a. talking with his colleagues
   b. eating *kanpyo* rolls
   c. cooking his dinner at home

2 以下はニュースの概要です。空所に適切な単語を書き入れましょう。語頭の文字（群）は与えてあります。

Kanpyo is made from a bottle gourd. Dried bottle gourds are often used as (**sp**   ¹)《複数形》or as musical (**in**   ²)《複数形》. *Kanpyo* is a well known (**in**   ³) in sushi rolls. In addition, it has been discovered that *kanpyo* can be used by medical (**in**   ⁴)《複 数 形》as artificial skin for practicing their suturing techniques. This is because the texture of *kanpyo* is similar to that of (**h**   ⁵) skin. Using *kanpyo* is very economical because Tochigi Prefecture produces almost all the bottle gourds in Japan.

3 CD の音声を聞いて、次ページ News Story の❶〜❼の文中にある空所に適切な単語を書き入れましょう。音声は２回繰り返されます。　　　　　　　　　◎ CD 29

Anchor: *Kanpyo*, an ingredient commonly used in sushi rolls, is a specialty of Tochigi Prefecture, north of Tokyo, which produces about 99 percent of it. ❶ Now, its new, (¹)

(²) (³) (⁴)

5   (⁵) (⁶). Let's find out more. This report was filmed in February.

❶ 予想外の使い
方がますます
関心を集めて
いる

Narrator: ❷ (¹) (²) (³)

(⁴) (⁵), coming from this speaker made of.... Here's a hint.

❷ くつろげるジ
ャズが流れる
カフェ

10 **Sushi chef:** (*He serves a dish to a customer.*) Your *kanpyo* roll.

Narrator: *Kanpyo* is made of a **bottle gourd**. Its fruit is the size of a basketball, and it's shaved and dried to use in cooking, especially sushi rolls. And now the gourd is being **harnessed** as speakers.

15 **Kashiwazaki Daichi (Manager, Cafe FUJINUMA):**

❸ (¹) (²) (³)

(⁴) (⁵) with a depth that **enhances** the music.

❸ それはすばら
しい音質を生
み出す

Narrator: Takahashi Akira, the president of a car stereo company,

20   came up with the idea after learning that gourds have been used as musical instruments around the world.

Takahashi Akira (President, sound tec, TAKAHASHI DENKI) :

❹ Gourds (¹) (²)

(³) (⁴) (⁵)

25   (⁶).

❹ 音を増幅させ
る特徴がある

Narrator: That's thanks to the **hollow** interior. And the cotton-like **fluffs** left inside absorb unwanted noise, resulting in clearer sound.

Kanpyo has found its way to another unusual application:

medicine. Interns are practicing skin **suturing** techniques. First, they spread out several-millimeter-thick **rehydrated** *kanpyo* **strips** and stretch until **taut**. ❺ (¹)
(²) (³) (⁴)
(⁵).

This *kanpyo* practice kit is the **brainchild** of Professor Mato Takashi.

Mato Takashi (Professor, Jichi Medical University): The idea struck [*me*]* when I was eating *kanpyo* at a sushi restaurant. It has a similar texture to human skin.

Narrator: Conventional kits run several hundred dollars, but using *kanpyo* significantly cuts cost, allowing more practice time for **aspiring** doctors.

Medical Student: It's springier than you might think on the outside, but when the needle **penetrates**, it gives you a sensation similar to the one that you get when suturing a person's skin.

Narrator: A medical equipment maker has set its eye on marketing the *kanpyo* practice kit.

Mato: ❻ I hope this kit will be used for training medical students and
(¹) (²) (³)
(⁴) (⁵) (⁶).

Narrator: *Kanpyo*, Tochigi's famous specialty. It's finding new uses beyond the **culinary** field. ❼ (¹)
(²) (³) (⁴)
(⁵) (⁶)?

❺ 彼らは人工的
な皮膚を作り
出したところ
だ

❻ 彼らが優れた
医師になるの
を助ける

❼ この控えめな
ひょうたんで
何ができるか

Note
＊ ふつうは me のような目的語を伴う

Review the Key Expressions

各問、選択肢から適切な単語を選び、英文を完成させましょう。なお、余分な単語が１語
ずつあります。

1. 警察はその逃亡者がどこに潜んでいたか、つきとめ [明らかにし] ようとしたが失敗した。

(   ) tried but (   ) to (_____) out (   )

the (   ) was (   ).

> where   hiding   failed   fugitive   find   impossible   police

2. みなさん、made of と made from の使い方の違いに注意しましょう。お酒は米から作
りますが、一方伝統的な机は木から作ります。

Class, note the difference in (   ) between *made of* and *made from*. Sake is

made (   ) (   ), whereas (   ) desks are made

(_____) (   ).

> wood   rice   traditional   in   of   from   usage

3. 最近多くの企業が、業務効率を改善しコストを削減する目的で、IT 関連の予算を増やした。

Many companies (   ) recently (   ) their IT-related

(   ) to (   ) business (   ) and (_____)

costs.

> cut   budgets   have   improve   increased   efficiency   rose

4. 池江璃花子選手は白血病から立ち直った後、五輪の水泳でメダルを獲ることを目標にした。

Ikee Rikako has (_____) her (_____) on (   ) an

Olympic medal in (   ) after (   ) from (   ).

> set   winning   leukemia   swimming   recovering   hospital   eyes

● Discussion Questions

1. What ethnic cuisine do you like best? Do you know how to prepare any dishes? Explain.

2. Would you like to become a medical doctor? Why? What field of work are you
interested in?

Lifesaver for Type 1 Diabetes Patients

1型糖尿病患者を救いたい

1型糖尿病患者のインスリン療法で、最も起こりやすい副作用が低血糖である。患者がそういう状態に陥ったとき、特別な訓練を受けた「低血糖アラート犬」がいれば、知らせてくれる。海外ではその養成・実用化が進んでおり患者の命を救った事例もあるが、日本ではまだ立ち遅れているのが現状である。

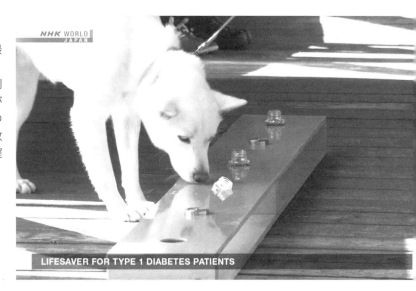

LIFESAVER FOR TYPE 1 DIABETES PATIENTS

● Words & Phrases

◎ CD 30

☐ **type 1 diabetes** 1型糖尿病

☐ to **afflict** （人など）を苦しめる

He was always *afflicted* with a sense of inferiority.

彼はいつも劣等感に苦しめられていた。

☐ **injection** 注射

☐ **insulin** インスリン〈cf. すい臓から血液内に分泌されるホルモン〉

☐ **hormone** ホルモン

☐ **side effect** （薬などの）副作用

☐ **consciousness** 意識

☐ to **detect** 〜を見つける、見抜く

☐ **diabetic** 糖尿病患者

Diabetics must follow a low-fat diet.

糖尿病患者は、低脂肪食事療法に従わなければならない。

☐ **undisciplined** 鍛えられていない

☐ **cursed** 呪われた

☐ **scent** におい、香り

Before You Watch

以下は、体調不良などに関する表現です。下の枠内から適切な単語を選び、空所に入れましょう。

1. ここ何日か体調がよくないです。
I've been under the (   ) for a few days.

2. 体調が悪いです。インフルエンザ（にかかった）かもしれません。
I'm in bad (   ). I think I'm coming down with the flu.

3. 体がだるいです。　I have no (   ).

4. 鼻水が出ます。　I have a (   ) nose.

5. 鼻が詰まっています。　I have a (   ) nose.

6. 少しめまいがします。　I'm a bit (   ).

7. 頭痛がします。　I have a (   ).

8. 熱があります。　I have a (   ).

9. お腹が痛いです。　I have a (   ).

10. 喉が痛いです。　I have a (   ) throat.

11. 下痢をしています。　I have (   ).

12. 便秘しています。　I'm (   ).

13. 腰が痛いです。　I have a (   ).

14. 少し吐き気がします。　I feel a bit (   ).

backache	constipated	diarrhea	dizzy	energy
fever	headache	nauseous	runny	shape
sore	stomachache	stuffy	weather	

Watch the News
First Viewing

ニュースを見て、内容と合っているものは T、違っているものは F を選びましょう。

1. Rian must get shots four times or more every day because of her diabetes.   [T / F]

2. Service dogs can tell if a patient has low blood sugar by looking at his/her face.   [T / F]

3. A Japanese NPO began training its first service dog starting this year.   [T / F]

1 ニュースをもう一度見て、各問の空所に入る適切な選択肢を a 〜 c から選びましょう。

1. Service dogs for diabetics are helping patients in ____.
   a. Russia and Asian countries
   b. North and South America
   c. Europe and North America

2. When the service dog Animo started to live with Rian, he seemed ____.
   a. to very quickly adjust to his new environment
   b. confused by the new smells around him
   c. happy with his new family and home

3. Animo ____.
   a. later alerted Rian about her low blood sugar
   b. never let Rian know about her blood sugar level
   c. needs much more training to become a service dog

2 以下の各情報を、ニュースに出てきた順序に並べましょう。

1. Eiichi Ohmura suffers from diabetes and faced discrimination.
2. Children with type 1 diabetes must have insulin shots that may cause side effects.
3. Rian is 11 years old and will probably live with type 1 diabetes all her life.
4. Service dogs overseas alert diabetics to avoid the danger of low blood sugar.

3 CD の音声を聞いて、次ページ News Story の❶〜❼の文中にある空所に適切な単語を書き入れましょう。音声は 2 回繰り返されます。　　　　　　◎ CD 31

Anchor: Many people may think of diabetes as a lifestyle disease that tends to affect seniors. But a more *rare** form of the illness **afflicts** patients when they're young, and the cause is unclear. NHK World's Cristel Bereder reports on a pioneering initiative to help those who are suffering from this condition here in Japan.

Narrator: Eleven-year-old Rian Tsukuda will probably have to live with type 1 diabetes for the rest of her life. That means she has to get **injections** at least four times a day. Her body cannot produce enough **insulin**, a **hormone** that regulates blood sugar.

The injections can cause serious **side effects**, including periods of dangerously low blood sugar. ❶ If the patient
(¹) (²) (³)
(⁴) (⁵) (⁶),
they can lose **consciousness** and even die. The disease can be particularly hard for children like Rian to manage. ❷ Family members (¹) (²)
(³) (⁴) (⁵)
(⁶) (⁷) their blood sugar, especially at night.

Kyoko Tsukuda: Most of the time my daughter sleeps right through without knowing whether she has low blood sugar, and that terrifies me.

Narrator: Service dogs are now helping patients like Rian in Europe and North America. ❸ The animals can **detect** whether someone has low blood sugar by the smell of their breath and
(¹) (²) (³)
(⁴) (⁵).

❶ 何か甘いもの
をすぐに食べ
ない（と）

❷ 〜に細心の注
意を払わなけ
ればならない

❸ 危険を避ける
ように彼らに
注意を喚起す
る

❹ While (¹) (²) (³) (⁴) (⁵) (⁶), that is about to change. An NPO that supports type 1 **diabetics** started training the service dogs here two years ago.

Eiichi Ohmura also suffers from the disease and launched the project after facing discrimination.

Eiichi Ohmura: People used to tell my family I was **undisciplined**, **cursed** or doomed. Alert dogs will help people understand that patients need injections every day to control their blood sugar.

Narrator: (*A dog is shown.*) This is their most successful student. His name is Animo, and he's undergone extensive coaching with the help of an expert from Sweden to detect the right **scent**.

❺ (¹) (²) (³) (⁴) (⁵), the next step begins in the real world.

He's sent to live with Rian for more than a week. She shows him her room, his workplace. The conditions are tougher because there are so many new smells. Will Animo be able to detect low blood sugar on Rian's breath? His training resumes in these new surroundings.

And just two nights later, Animo successfully alerts Rian.

Rian Tsukuda: ❻ He's like (¹) (²) (³) (⁴) (⁵) (⁶). He feels like family.

Narrator: Animo looks set to become Japan's first diabetes alert dog. ❼ It's a small step but could lead to big changes (¹) (²) (³) (⁴) (⁵) . Cristel Bereder, NHK World.

❹ 日本にはまだ
　　いない

❺ 基本的な訓練
　　を終えたあと
　　で

❻ 私の命を守る
　　英雄（のよう
　　な）

❼ 全国の患者さ
　　んたちのため
　　に

Note

＊ rarer が正しい形

Review the Key Expressions

各問、選択肢から適切な単語を選び、英文を完成させましょう。なお、余分な単語が1語ずつあります。

1. 首都圏のアパートは家賃が高い傾向にあるが、探し続ければもっと妥当なものが見つかるだろう。

Apartments in the (　　　　　　) area (　　　　　　　) (　　　　　　　) be more expensive to (　　　　　　), but we can find more (　　　　) ones if we keep (　　　　).

> rent　metropolitan　to　than　looking　tend　reasonable

2. ジョンの今の貯蓄率では、たぶん一生ずっと働かなければならないだろう。

(　　　　　) by John's (　　　　　) rate of (　　　　　), he will probably have to (　　　　) for the (　　　　　) of (　　　　) (　　　　　).

> current　rest　work　savings　judging　his　life　task

3. その司書は、学生たちの論文のテーマに関する文献の検索を手伝ってくれた。

The librarian (　　　　　　) (　　　　　) (　　　　　) (　　　　　) the books (　　　　) the themes of their (　　　　).

> on　helped　papers　students　refer　for　look

4. ジムの態度が一変し［変化を経験し］て、最近ずっと友好的になった。

Jim (　　　　　) (　　　　　　) a change in (　　　　　) and has (　　　　) (　　　　) friendlier (　　　　).

> become　undergone　has　recently　attitude　more　much

● Discussion Questions

1. How long would you like to live? What would you like to do most during your life? Explain.

2. What pets do you like best: dogs, cats or some other animals? Why?

このテキストのメインページ
www.kinsei-do.co.jp/plusmedia/41

次のページの QR コードを読み取る
直接ページにジャンプできます

オンライン映像配信サービス「plus⁺Media」について

本テキストの映像は plus⁺Media ページ（www.kinsei-do.co.jp/plusmedia）から、ストリーミング再生でご利用いただけます。手順は以下に従ってください。

ログインページ

ログイン

● ご利用には、ログインが必要です。
サイトのログインページ（www.kinsei-do.co.jp/plusmedia/login）へ行き、plus⁺Media パスワード（次のページのシールをはがしたあとに印字されている数字とアルファベット）を入力します。

● パスワードは各テキストにつき1つです。
有効期限は、はじめてログインした時点から1年間になります。

[利用方法]

次のページにある QR コード、もしくは plus⁺Media トップページ（www.kinsei-do.co.jp/plusmedia）から該当するテキストを選んで、そのテキストのメインページにジャンプしてください。

メニューページ　　　再生画面

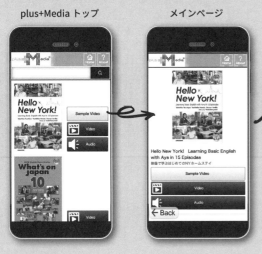

plus+Media トップ　　　メインページ

「Video」「Audio」をタッチすると、それぞれのメニューページにジャンプしますので、そこから該当する項目を選べば、ストリーミングが開始されます。

[推奨環境]

iOS (iPhone, iPad)	OS: iOS 12 以降 ブラウザ：標準ブラウザ	Android	OS: Android 6 以降 ブラウザ：標準ブラウザ、Chrome
PC	OS: Windows 7/8/8.1/10, MacOS X　ブラウザ：Internet Explorer 10/11, Microsoft Edge, Firefox 48以降, Chrome 53以降, Safari		

※最新の推奨環境についてはウェブサイトをご確認ください。
※上記の推奨環境を満たしている場合でも、機種によってはご利用いただけない場合もあります。また、推奨環境は技術動向等により変更される場合があります。予めご了承ください。

本書には音声 CD（別売）があります

NHK NEWSLINE 5

映像で学ぶ NHK 英語ニュースが伝える日本 5

2022年1月20日　初版第1刷発行
2024年3月30日　初版第5刷発行

編著者　　山　﨑　達　朗
　　　　Stella M. Yamazaki
発行者　　福　岡　正　人
発行所　　株式会社　金星堂
（〒101-0051）東京都千代田区神田神保町 3-21
Tel. (03) 3263-3828 （営業部）
　　 (03) 3263-3997 （編集部）
Fax (03) 3263-0716
http://www.kinsei-do.co.jp

編集担当　稲葉真美香　　　　　Printed in Japan
印刷所・製本所／大日本印刷株式会社

ISBN978-4-7647-4144-7 C1082